# Creating
# Convincing
# Characters

# Creating
# Convincing
# Characters

Nicholas Corder

**COMPASS
BOOKS**

Winchester, UK
Washington, USA

First published by Compass Books, 2014
Compass Books is an imprint of John Hunt Publishing Ltd., Laurel House, Station Approach,
Alresford, Hants, SO24 9JH, UK
office1@jhpbooks.net
www.johnhuntpublishing.com
www.compass-books.net

For distributor details and how to order please visit the 'Ordering' section on our website.

Text copyright: Nicholas Corder 2013

ISBN: 978 1 78279 164 5

A CIP catalogue record for this book is available from the British Library.

Design: Stuart Davies


Printed and bound by CPI Group (UK) Ltd, Croydon, CR0 4YY

We operate a distinctive and ethical publishing philosophy in all
areas of our business, from our global network of authors to
production and worldwide distribution.

# CONTENTS

Acknowledgements                                                    vi

Introduction                                                         1

Preface: The boys watch the girls while the girls
   watch the boys ...                                                2

Chapter 1: Why are characters so important?                          6

Chapter 2: The character questionnaire                              12

Chapter 3: Walk-on parts and minor players                          22

Chapter 4: Character actors and major stars                         30

Chapter 5: What can we steal? Using real people                     40

Chapter 6: What can we steal? Types, archetypes
   and stereotypes                                                  49

Chapter 7: What can we steal? Birth signs and bumps                 59

Chapter 8: What can we steal? Learning from psychologists
   and psychopaths                                                  65

Chapter 9: Introducing a character                                  74

Chapter 10: Character in action – why showing is better
   than telling                                                     85

Chapter 11: What makes him tick? Character motivation               92

Chapter 12: Making your characters talk                             99

Chapter 13: What does your character think (and how
   does she think it?)                                             117

Chapter 14: Who's telling the story? Point-of-view
   and voice                                                       125

Chapter 15: Your character and their world                         147

Chapter 16: A rose by any other name                               159

Chapter 17: The villain of the piece                               168

Postscript                                                         177

Bibliography                                                       179

# Acknowledgements

I'd like to thank all the writers and students whose ideas have gone into the melting pot over the years. I've been lucky enough to work in a vast range of settings — prisons, community centres, schools, libraries, universities, adult education classes, the National Health Service. You can learn so much from mixing with writers at all stages of their development. Thanks also to the writers whose brains I picked.

Special thanks as ever, to my long-suffering wife, Pauline, who made coffee, sandwiches and intelligent suggestions as this book stumbled towards completion.

# Introduction

Thank you for buying this book or for borrowing it from the library. I hope you find it useful.

Character is everything in fiction. You'll have your own favourites, from literature as well as TV and films. Some of these may be comic, some tragic. Above all, they will be people who make you feel some great emotion.

This book is about creating characters for fiction writers. It assumes that you're probably aiming to write short stories or a novel. Of course, many of the ideas in it can be used in scriptwriting for the stage or the screen and I'm sure that if that is your intention, then you'll be able to pick the relevant bits and use them.

This book aims to get you thinking about how to create characters, what readers are likely to think about your characters and the various techniques that go into getting your characters across to the reader.

There are various exercises at the end of each section. Please feel free to do them or ignore them or to replace them with ideas of your own. Remember that a writing exercise is precisely what it says. It's an exercise; it's not the real thing. But all professional athletes limber up before a race.

Above all, have fun.

# Preface: The boys watch the girls while the girls watch the boys...

*Sit in a café, take a trip on a bus or a train. Look at the people sitting near you. Look at their clothes and hair, the book they're reading, the game they're playing, the person they're travelling with. Look at what they're carrying – shopping bags, supermarkets' plastic carriers, brief-cases, lap-tops, rucksacks, hand luggage, big suitcases.*

*Now start guessing.*

*What do they do for a living? Where were they last night? How much money do they have in the bank? What's in their handbag/wallet? Who is the person with them? What do they feel about them? Or why are they travelling/eating/drinking alone? Where are they going to after they've had their drink/sandwich/meal or when the bus/train/plane gets to its destination?*

There's nothing much more pleasurable than people-watching. A bit of minor snooping, mixed in with some casual eavesdropping and shaken together with a huge dollop of specu-lation, is immensely rewarding for the writer.

Sometimes, it's just little snippets that you can store in your notebook for the future — snatches of dialogue that you reckon might come in handy. Indeed, the modern use of mobile phones means that there is always a store of gems to be salted away:

The offended lover. 'I told him if he was going to be like that, he could be like that, and that's that.'

*What was he being like? And might someone else prefer it?*

The disappointed job-hunter. 'They said I was too young for it, but my date of birth's on my CV, so you'd think they'd have read that... I think they tell you anything. So I was just going to have a cup of tea, but I'm going to have cake as well and they can pay for that too.'

*The person from Human Resources, who seems on-the-ball to her colleagues, but is thoughtlessly mucking up young people's lives through low-level incompetence. And what's worse, the job hunter had only got two interviews and they were both on the same day, but had chosen this one as the likelier bet.*

The geographically-challenged Londoner. 'We're just coming into Crewe, so we can only be a couple of minutes from Manchester.'

*Wouldn't you just love to send him on a team-building exercise that involved orienteering? Perhaps we could send the lady from Human Resources as well.*

Everywhere around us, there are people who make us wonder about their lives, who seem to have hidden stories that we can use. People-watch and you begin to see how you can use complete strangers to populate a story.

I was once on a boat crossing the English Channel, returning from a holiday in France. It was one of those high-speed affairs where you have to book a reclining seat. The boat was at best half-full. We had a row of comfy recliners all to ourselves, as did the couple behind us. They were the kind of people who talk too loudly, not so as to gain the attention of people around them, but because they lacked self-awareness. I suspect they always had the radio and the telly on too loudly as well. They had quite obviously grown used to one another over time. Both of them spoke a version of that hard-to-place accent which seems now to have the label of Estuary English, although he sounded a couple of notches posher than she did.

What intrigued me more than their slightly mismatched accents were the components of their conversation. For a long time, they talked about various high-ranking politicians from within the British Conservative party. They talked about them in such a way that they obviously encountered them frequently, heard them speak, saw them having a drink. The couple weren't boasting, they were simply doling out some pretty anodyne gossip. X didn't like white wine; he preferred red. Y had been let down by a baby-sitter.

At this point, my guess was that they were members of the Tory party, the kind who attend the annual conferences and possibly go to dinners on the rubber-chicken circuit. But, then as the conversation wore on, they began to concentrate on just one Member of Parliament. Was our rear-side neighbour perhaps the local party agent?

They chatted away as people do, of cars, conservatories and possible new furniture. I hazarded that they were a bit nouveau-riche. If he was the party agent, then maybe he'd had a successful business career and built up a portfolio of car sales rooms, which he'd now passed on to the next generation. She'd raised the family, who'd all joined the business now and together they were spending an active early retirement canvassing for their party of choice.

Because of the headrests, it was tricky to take a look at them without making it entirely obvious that I was utterly nosy, possibly to the point of certifiability.

But I knew they'd be tanned the colour of builders' tea. He would have his shirt open a button too far and be wearing some kind of grey or light tan shoes, possibly with some little tassels on them. He'd be the kind of man who, when he's had a drink too many, backs hairy arts students into a corner by the bar and prods them in the chest whilst telling them all about the importance of being a self-made man. Later, he'll confess that he doesn't know much about art, but he knows what he likes. She would be wearing a scoop-neck T-shirt, possibly with a few rhinestones on it, but certainly with a logo or a designer name emblazoned across her chest. The T-shirt would reveal a cleavage burnt the colour of roast chicken. Her wrists would be circled in bangles, her fingers weighed down by a shop-window's worth of over-priced gemstones. Yes, they would be dripping in obvious signs of newly-acquired wealth.

When I got out of the seat, I took a quick peek. Bitter disappointment, but a lesson in stereotyping. None of my preconceived (and obviously prejudiced) ideas was right. They turned out to be a rather badly-dressed, middle-aged couple. His trousers were not quite long enough, so flapped mid-calf, revealing socks and sandals. She was tanned, as one might be from a few hours in the sun, but nothing more. She wore a plain one-coloured summer dress. They were both the kind of people you'd never look at twice if you passed them in the street unless you're one of those socks-sandals combination spotters.

Later, the talk turned to her place of work and it soon became obvious from her conversation that she worked in a supermarket stacking shelves. It still wasn't entirely clear what he did for a living, but the conversation rattled between political tittle-tattle and the most effective way to re-stock the beer, wines and spirits aisle, which wasn't the way the supervisor insisted it be done. Bizarrely, during all this, there was not one actual political opinion expressed. For people who seemed to know a lot of politicians, they didn't seem to talk a lot of politics.

I've never used this couple in a story, or a play, but have always been intrigued by them. They weren't doing high-profile boasting, like those businessmen on trains who snarl into their mobile phones. *'They need to know we're serious, Jeff. It's 250 K or we walk.'* (If they're that important, why are they in cattle class with us plebs?) They weren't getting drunk and revealing secrets, like a latter-day Martha and George. They weren't slashing the seats, failing to supervise children or breaking wind uncontrollably.

I was intrigued by them, and remain so today. There were so many contradictions between appearance, work and the subject of their conversation that I'd just love to know more about them. Of course, it's unlikely that I ever will, unless, of course, I start making it all up...

# 1

# Why are characters so important?

Let's take one of the great literary creations, Sherlock Holmes. You may not be a fan — it doesn't matter. The point is that he's well-known. What's the first thing that comes to mind when we think about him? The deer-stalker hat or the calabash pipe? Or could it be the violin-playing or the opium-taking? Maybe it's some of his choicer quotations: 'The game's afoot!' or 'Elementary, my dear Watson.' Or 'When you have eliminated all which is impossible, then whatever remains, however improbable, must be the truth.' Maybe it's his Baker Street lodgings, or the voice of his admiring companion Dr. Watson.

Unless you're a big Sherlock Holmes fan, I suspect that you'd be hard put to remember any of his cases in great detail.

This is strange. The solving of the crime is a crucial element of detective fiction, but despite this, it isn't the stories we remember — the cases solved and the loose ends tied up — but the detectives themselves. It is Holmes, Maigret, Poirot, Morse, Wallander or Miss Marple who stay in our imaginations. To be fair, I suspect that for most of us, our mental pictures of these characters are based on what we've seen on the screen, rather than read on the page. Indeed, the calabash pipe and the deerstalker aren't derived directly from Conan Doyle's stories, but from various portrayals of the detective. 'Elementary, my dear Watson' was only ever said on film as well. But the point remains — we remember the characters long after the storylines have dissolved and gone to join the gloopy soup that is all of those things of which we have only some distant recollection.

Characters are crucial. We don't become emotionally involved in a story unless we can see a human being at the core of an event. This holds for life just as it does for art. Whilst we might turn up our noses at the flimsy supermarket magazines that feature juicy snippets about TV semi-stars or minor celebrities, we should also be aware that it's not just the tabloids who are obsessed with individuals. The serious press is also fixated with them. It's just that your Sunday broadsheet will be likely to interview a film director, a writer, a musician or someone considered a little less frivolous. From fatuous reality-TV celeb to major composer, you're still reading about people, though.

On Boxing Day 2004, an underwater earthquake off the coast of Sumatra caused tidal waves up to 100 feet high that crashed along the coasts of Indonesia, Sri Lanka, India, Thailand, The Maldives and several other countries. The death toll has been estimated at around 230,000. To give some idea of scale, that's roughly the population of Derby or Stoke-on-Trent or Southampton in the UK. The equivalent in the USA would be Jersey, New Jersey or Lincoln, Nebraska; in Australia: Wollongong, in New Zealand: Hamilton. It's a lot of people. It defies imagination. It's too big for us to understand. To bring human scale to this, when the newspapers reported this tragedy, they often focused on individual stories. This isn't because the media didn't care about the other 229, 999 people, but that when we read about disasters such as this, our sympathies are set in motion by understanding what has happened to a person or a small group. We can identify with a small number of people, we can't conceive of the larger numbers.

Although it may sound almost too obvious to spell out, let's do it anyway.

*People want to read about people.*

Even if we're dealing with ideas about politics and philosophy, we need what Robert McKee calls 'the seductive emotions of art'. What would you rather watch? House of Commons TV debating changes to the Dangerous Dogs Act or a TV drama in which a genuinely caring dog owner finds that his dog has slipped the leash and savaged a child, only to find that the child's father is now after his blood?

And the most seductive emotion, for any writer of fiction or drama is conveyed through the characters he or she creates. Character is king. Good, strong, passionate, interesting, human characters allow us to identify with the people we are reading about or watching on screen. As Sandra Newman and Howard Mittelmark say in their wonderful *How Not to Write a Novel*, if you want to make a book unreadable, 'populate it with boring, unbelievable and unpleasant characters.' In the example of the dangerous dogs above, I deliberately made the owner of the dog a decent guy, because a head-case with a 90-kilo Japanese Tosa Inu fighting dog has few sympathies, save amongst fellow head-cases who own 90-kilo Japanese Tosa Inu fighting dogs.

Occasionally, someone breaks with the centrality of character and is temporarily successful. For instance, in the 1930s, the playwright Bertholt Brecht developed the *Verfremdungseffekt*, usually referred to in English as the alienation effect (or sometimes as distancing effect). Brecht's idea was that he wanted a kind of separation, between the audience and the action that takes place on the stage, an awareness that they weren't watching something real, but created by a writer, director, actors, stage designers, musicians. He saw audience identification with character as facile. If the audience become too involved in the characters they are watching, then they are merely being entertained (and that would never do). If he moved beyond simple entertainment, then they would be engaged on an intellectual level with the politics of the play. And Brecht felt duty-bound to educate the theatre-goer.

The strange thing is that those Brecht plays that seem to have lasted well, such as *Mother Courage and Her Children* or *The Life of Galileo*, have strong central characters. It may be the case that we, as readers and viewers, will try to identify with someone, no matter what the writer throws at us. We need good characters as a compass by which to steer.

Characters are important as they are the means by which we become involved in the action of a story. By *action*, I don't necessarily mean that of high-paced thrillers, such as shoot-outs or burning cars, but the *events* of a story. In all the great classics that have survived the decades, or even centuries, we want to root for our great characters. We want Robinson Crusoe to find a way off his desert island, whilst marvelling at his ingenuity; we're rooting for Elizabeth Bennet to choose Mr. Darcy; we're aching for Yossarian to escape the madness of war. Even if you want to write highly political material — books that will change the world — you still have to think about having great characters. Harper Lee's *To Kill a Mockingbird*, which is as important a social statement as anything ever written, is carried by the voice of Scout and the great characters who parade through the book — Boo Radley, Calpurnia, Atticus Finch. Without them, the impact of the book would have been severely weakened — it would have turned into political tub-thumping. As it is, it is far more subtle and persuasive. If people want to have political ideas rammed down their throats, then they can always hang around Speakers' Corner in Hyde Park or watch a Michael Moore documentary. George Orwell's political criticisms, *1984* and *Animal Farm*, might by now long have disappeared from bookshops if they had been nonfiction. They need that human (or quasi-human) element to carry the reader.

As readers we like to identify, or at least empathise, with characters. We like to share their joys, feel the same fears and rejections and bruises. We like to root for them or try to understand them. And even when we know that the character will always succeed — such as with James Bond or Sherlock Holmes (Reichenbach Falls excepted), then we want to know what cleverness they're going to use to unmask the villain whilst keeping all their body parts.

## Where do characters come from?

The writing life would be so simple if there were such a thing as a character creation machine that could do it all for you. Unfortunately, as John Braine says, 'there is no formula for character creation.' It's a pity, as it would make the writer's lot far easier. You could simply pull out your recipe card and on it would be written some kind of formula:

16% you, the writer, with all your foibles and fancies, tastes and prejudices

5% childhood memories, especially the unpleasant ones

17% your next-door neighbour

10% the woman you argued with in the supermarket car-park

12% Arm-pit Armstrong, the man who taught you geography at school and on whom you need to exact revenge

9% pure invention from looking down a list of adjectives of personal quality

15% the results of a dream you had last night

12% stolen from a Chekhov short story

4% induced by drinking too much caffeine whilst writing

Not only is there no neat recipe, but if you were to pick half-a-dozen writers at random, they would all use different approaches. There would also be some kind of overlap of all the dozens of techniques, but if you attempted to create a Venn diagram, it would probably look like an accident with a spirograph and an ink bottle.

Authors don't use one single method for creating characters, but build up a set of techniques over the years, so that eventually, they probably don't even know how they're doing it. What's more, they might not even dare to think openly about how they do it for fear of losing 'the magic'.

However, all of them will go through many of the methods described in this book, even if they do it subconsciously. So what we're going to do in the following pages is look at a variety of different sources, methods and ideas for how we can start creating characters, and more importantly, how we can make those characters feel like real people.

Some of these techniques may appeal to you. Others may leave you cold. Your task is to cherry-pick what you find most useful and you will eventually begin honing your own method or even methods of character creation. You may perhaps develop new ways not even mentioned in these pages, so that if you too were asked how you do it, you'd be hard put to explain the process.

We're going to start with an old-fashioned character questionnaire, just so as to flag up some of the things you need to be thinking about as you try to get the people on your pages to take flight and exist not only in your own head, but the imaginations of your readers. But before we do this, here's a little exercise. There are several of them scattered throughout the book. Please feel free to do them, or ignore them.

## Over to you

Think back to your school days. Choose two teachers, one of whom you really liked, the other someone you didn't get on with. Write a couple of paragraphs on each of them, describing what they were like and why you preferred one to the other.

# 2

# The character questionnaire

Many books on creative writing include checklists as a means of helping you to create character. This one is no exception. I've tried to make this questionnaire as full as possible within the constraints of the book.

I've spoken to several writers about the subject of character charts, inventories and questionnaires. Nobody I spoke to actually works through any kind of tick-list or fills out a form. However, importantly, they all agreed that the kinds of ingredients given in such lists can help the thought-process; they prompt the writer to think about different aspects of the people in their imaginary worlds.

It's probably best to view what follows in the next few pages as a series of nudges and reminders, rather than some virtual interview. It's also entirely possible to answer a questionnaire such as this and still not end up with a convincing character. Here goes:

## Name

What is your character's name? In full.

Do they have any nicknames? How did they come by these? What do they think of these nicknames, are they unpleasant or flattering?

What do other characters in your story refer to them as?

What do they think about their name? Do they ever wish they'd been called something else? Do they leave bits of it out?

Have they changed their name at all? Through marriage? To hide something?

If they have a title (Sir, Lord, Baroness, Professor ...), do they use it or prefer not to? Or do they use it when they think it might be handy?

# Age

How old are they?

What is their date of birth?

What sign of the zodiac are they? Do they attach any importance to this? Do they read their horoscope? If so, do they believe it?

Are they happy with the age they are now? Would they prefer to be older/younger?

Do they look their age? Dress appropriately for it?

# General Appearance

How tall are they? Would they like to be taller/shorter?

How much do they weigh? Are they overweight, underweight, very muscly, scrawny, burly, doll-like, squat, athletic?

What do they think about their weight? Are they unhappy/happy/unbothered?

What colour hair do they have? Is it natural/dyed?

What colour are their eyes?

Do they have any scars? If so, how did they get them?

Do they have any particular tics, habits or mannerisms?

How do they dress? Smart/scruffy/expensive/designer/charity shop/cast-offs?

Do they care about the way they dress? Do they like to dress up for special occasions?

Do they wear any jewellery?

Do they have any tattoos?

If you were going to point them out in a crowded room, how would you describe them?

# Speech

How articulate are they?

Do they say a lot or a little?

Do they speak with a regional accent? If so, how broad? Have they changed the way they speak?

What is their tone of voice like? Wheedling, persuasive, even, shouty?

Is their voice high- or low-pitched?

Is English (assuming you're writing in English) their first language? Are they an immigrant/emigrant?

Do they have pet sayings or expressions?

## At home

Where were they born?

Where do they live now?

Did they move here from another part of the country? From abroad? Are they born and bred in this place/area?

What kind of an area is it socially? Is it rural, suburban or urban? Is the general area unkempt, pristine, up-and-coming, due for slum clearance?

What kind of a house or apartment is it?

What are the furniture, ornaments, pictures, books, CDs, films, gadgetry, etc. in the house?

Did they inherit furniture, pictures, etc.? If not, where did they buy them?

How would a prospective purchaser evaluate the property? How would an estate agent describe it?

Who lives at the same address? Do they have family/flat-mates/lodger/landlord? How do they get on?

Do they have pets? Do others in the household have pets? Do they like them? Would they like a pet if they haven't got one or do they wish they kept a different kind of pet?

Do they get on with their neighbours? Why/why not?

Which room do they like to spend time in – kitchen/study /bedroom/TV lounge/garage/shed?

Do they like living where they do? What would they change? Where would they rather live?

## World of work

What job do they do?

How do they feel about what they do? Does it thrill/bore/feel useful/pointless?

Are they well/badly paid?

Do they feel (under)valued?

How do they get on with colleagues/boss/subordinates? Who do they talk to at work? Who do they avoid at work?

What does their desk/pigeon-hole/locker/cloakroom look like?

Are they a planner? Or do they go with the flow?

Do they spend their time at work avoiding work or working hard?

Are they good at their work, or overlooked or over-promoted?

What about past jobs? Were they happier before, or do they feel as though they're better off now? Were they something glamorous in a past life?

What would their CV look like? How truthful would it be?

Would they rather be doing something else? What? Why?

How do they get to work?

What impact does their job have on the people around them?

Do they manage to hang on to most of the money they make or do they have it spent well before the next pay day (spender or saver)?

## Transport

Can they drive?

Do they like driving? Are they any good at it? Do they think they're better than they are? Would they stand a chance of passing their test if they took it again now?

Do they own their own transport? Car/motorbike/bike? If so, is it the best money could buy, some heap of rusted junk or something middling? Be specific.

If they own a car or van, what is it like inside? Clean or full of old fish-and-chip wrappers, drinks cartons and sweet papers? Bumper stickers? St Christopher? Car fresheners?

Do they like their mode of transport? How important is it to them? Is it a status symbol or just a means of getting from A to B. Would they like to change their vehicle? If so, for what? How would you feel if they offered to give you a lift? Or do they travel by public transport? If so, how do they feel about this? Do they have to cram into hot underground trains or do they enjoy a suburban bus ride? Do they resent not owning a car, or do they feel they're doing their bit for the environment?

## Health

Are they in good health?

Do they have any illnesses or disabilities? If so, how do these affect their daily lives?

What is their attitude to any medical condition – stoicism or constant moaning?

What medicines/medical procedures are involved?

Do they believe in alternatives to proven medicine?

## Family

Are they single/married/divorced/widowed?

Are they looking for Mr/Miss Right? Or which marriage are they on? Who shares their bed?

If they have children, what is their attitude to parenting? Liberal/strict?

If they don't have children is that a deliberate choice or medical bad luck?

Do they have brothers & sisters? What is their place in the family? (e.g. eldest/middle/youngest child).

What is the worst thing they ever did to a sibling as a child? And the worst thing one of their siblings did to them?

Did they have a teddy? What was it called?

Are their parents alive or dead? What kind of a relationship do they/did they have? Names, if they're relevant.

Did they know their grandparents? Are they in touch with wider family?

What is their family's status? Where would they come on official social scales, such as the National Readership Survey (which classifies A — E)? Is their own status at odds with the rest of the family, e.g. dropout or self-made millionaire?

Who are they closest to in their family?

## Education

School/college/university? Do they value education? Is their education different to the rest of family?

Who was their favourite teacher?

What was their favourite subject?

Which lessons did they dread?

Who gave them the best advice when they were young?

## Religion

Do they believe in anything? Mainstream religion or alternative?

Are they regular/occasional attenders at a place of worship?

How important is it to them?

Do they believe in an after-life?

What do they think of people whose religious views differ from theirs?

What would they like their own funeral to look like?

## Political beliefs

What do they think of politicians in general? Their MP? The Mayor?

Are they a floating voter or party member?

How did they vote in the last election? Did they vote at all?

How strong are their beliefs? Are they a campaigner? Would they die for a belief?

What is their stance on hunting, capital punishment, prison sentencing, the education system?

What would they do to make their country better?

## Social life and interests

What do they like doing? Do they like sport/reading/ music/dance/cinema/fell-walking/cinema? Do they get to do it often? How good are they at it?

Who are their friends? Do they have a best friend? Who would they chat over any problems with?

Do they belong to any clubs/groups/associations?

## Favourites

What's their favourite colour?

What do they like best if they go out for a meal?

What's their favourite comfort food?

Do they have a favourite chair or place to sit?

What music do they listen to at home? In the car?

What's their favourite TV programme?

What's their favourite film?

Who do they most like spending time with?

What's their favourite book? Or do they prefer magazines?

What newspaper do they buy if any?

How do they like spending Sunday morning? Friday night?

What would be a treat for them?

If they went on *Desert Island Discs*, what would they choose as their luxury item?

If you were their friend, what would you buy them as a present?

## Inner life, general morality

Do they have a motto?

What is the most important lesson they have learned in life?

What is the best/worst thing we could say about this person?

What is the best/worst trait they could pass on to a child?

What are they afraid of?

Does anything keep them awake at night?

Have they ever been in trouble with the police?

Have they got enemies or rivals or people standing in their way?

What's the cause of this?
What would they never do?

## Motivation

What does this person want? What is missing from their life? How far are they prepared to go to get it?

## The film of the book

Who would you cast in the film of your story or novel?

## What the reader thinks

What will make the reader like/dislike this character?
What will make the reader root for this character? Or hope this character gets their just deserts?
What will make the reader remember this character?

## The Chinese portrait

Here's another approach to character questionnaires, which forces you to think about your characters in a slightly different light. This time, we're asking the question, 'how would you describe a person if you had to talk about them metaphorically?' In our everyday speech, we frequently use metaphors to describe people, often these are animal metaphors:

- His wife is a real cow.
- He's a stud.
- Her mother was a mousy woman.
- He's an ass.

So what we're doing here is thinking about a character in terms of something else. If this character were a car, what kind of car would they be? Not what kind of car would they drive, but what make would best represent them as a person? Would they be some sleek, sophisticated luxury marque with deep-padded leather seats? Or perhaps some nippy little red sports coupé with shiny chrome bumpers. Or maybe they'd be some uninsured rust-bucket, with 180,000 miles on the clock, which leaks oil, has a dodgy head gasket and is held together by road dirt and gaffer tape.

Or if this character were a chair, would they be some well-worn leather library arm-chair, where the stuffing is escaping from the arms, a bentwood chair that automatically demands rigid posture, or maybe a Roman triclinium or a plush crimson chaise longue?

## Over to you

1. Run through the checklist above, thinking about a character you have in mind, jotting rough notes as you go. Then write 300-500 words describing how your character spends a typical day.

2. Let's draw a Chinese portrait. Take a character you're working on (or the same character from Exercise 1) and try to think of him or her in metaphorical ways. If this character were a/an .................. what kind of ............ would they be?
   - Animal
   - Book or film
   - Colour
   - Dance
   - Dish in a restaurant
   - Drink
   - Historical character
   - Item of clothing
   - Item of footwear
   - Metal
   - Musical instrument
   - Part of the body
   - Piece of furniture

- Piece of music
- Place
- Residential area
- Season
- Sport or game
- Weapon
- Work of art

# 3

# Walk-on parts and minor players

Watch most films as the acting credits are rolling and, unless it's a listing in order of appearance, the actor with the biggest part will normally get top billing, followed by the supporting cast, all the way down to characters who aren't even allowed the luxury of names: 1st Dancing Girl, Drunk Student, Flatulent Lift Operator...

## Bit players

If all you need to do is have a character bring in a cup of coffee, or deliver the mail, then these are your bit-players, your walk-on parts. In a film or a TV series, they wouldn't even get to say anything, so that the producers can get away with hiring a 'background artist' (an extra), rather than having to pay for an actor who is going to speak and thus cost more to employ.

As a writer, you realise that these characters must be of only fleeting interest to the reader. To make sure this happens, it's best not to give such characters a name. In a book, and especially a short story, the moment you give a character a name, you give them some kind of importance in the reader's imagination.

If all the waiter in your story does is bring coffee, then we don't need to know anything more about him than the fact he brings coffee. For the sake of a bit of local colour, you might want to dress him up in black tie and dab some cologne behind his ears if the café is particularly expensive. At the other end of the scale, we might give him an egg-stained apron as with one oil-grimed hand he slops a mug of instant onto the Formica top, right next to the tomato-shaped ketchup bottle, whilst sneezing into his other. But essentially, we need no more than the externals unless the waiter is going to play some significant part. Indeed, build these characters up too much and we expect to see them again later in much the same way as when they cast a big name character actor/famous face in a film and they appear only fleetingly early on, you know for sure you'll see more of them.

If you have a character who is purely functional, make sure they are definitely in the background, or bite the bullet and just write them out completely. Do we actually need to see the cup of coffee being brought in, or can we begin the scene with our two main characters already sitting in the café, china cups or chipped mugs in hand?

## Minor characters and why they're so great for a writer

Here, we're dealing with characters who are important to the plot of a story, but don't have much else to do.

Minor characters are vital. Whilst you may not spend as much time thinking about them as you will your big players, they still have to convince the reader. A good minor character can perform a huge range of useful tasks and it is where E. M. Forster's idea of 'flat' characters – ones that stay the same throughout the story — can come in very handy.

Flat characters are often basic types: aggressive salesmen, predatory divorcées, flustered clerks, officious door-men, ladettes ... whatever. All of these types (or stereotypes) pepper any form of longer writing. They are not the characters who will be wiser or lonelier or more loved-up or more bitter as a result of their experience. These are not the kinds of characters that need to be fully-fledged creations on whom you have pages and pages of notes. But they are worth thinking through, so that not all your minor players come from the same identikit parade.

## Minor characters as plot disguisers

But here's a neat trick. You can create minor characters to help advance plot elements. By making the character a little colourful, you can disguise a plot point so that the reader takes it in without being aware of it.

Let's imagine that we need to establish that the house where our protagonist lives has an old-fashioned coal-hole as this is where the would-be murderer hides out later on in the book.

Obviously, we want to sew this information in early, so that we don't have to explain the sudden appearance of a coal-cellar just as the murderer jumps up, a cut-throat razor in his sooty hands.

Of course, we could simply send our protagonist down into the coal-cellar to fetch fuel for the fire. This would be fine, but a bit dull. It feels like a non-scene and we stand the danger of having the protagonist merely giving us some kind of boring internal monologue whilst she does it. (*It's all very well having a coal-fire, but decent central heating ... blah, blah, blah*). We could also have a throw-away line somewhere in a conversation: '*Oh, I won't be cold, there's plenty of coal down in the cellar.*'

But we can be wilier than this and use it as a chance to explore our main character in a full set-piece scene. Having another person come into the story gives us the possibility of an encounter, rather than staying inside the head of our protagonist.

We therefore decide to have a coal-merchant. However, if all he does is turn up, deliver the coal and do his best Dick-van-Dyke-Cockney (*Gor lumme, missus, them sacks ain't half heavy, stone the crows*), then again we've got a page or two that seemingly leads us nowhere.

Let's just flesh him out a little. All we need to do is give him a touch of character, some hints of a personality, then we can build a bit of a scene around him and, more importantly, we can make the encounter between him and the protagonist tell us something about our leading lady – we get to see her in a certain light, which allows the reader to understand her more fully. Perhaps she isn't very good at dealing with conflict. In which case, we could set one up.

Maybe we could make the coal-merchant rip her off in some

way. He delivers a bag too few. He charges more than he'd told her he would on the phone. When she realises this has happened, your protagonist has to deal with it in some way that will tell either the reader that she can't face up to a minor conflict, or it gives her an opportunity to start toughening up. Perhaps she runs after his lorry and blocks the way or if she discovers it later, she picks up the phone and argues with him. No matter what we decide, we've at least put her into a scene where we can find out more about her.

As a result, we've hidden the plot-point detail of the coal-cellar and given ourselves a chance to look at her character in more detail. As for the coal-merchant — all we know is that he's a low-level rip-off artist. But at least we know he's something more than just the coal-man. We can give him a few character-istics that stop him being an entire stereotype. Maybe he has a teddy bear on the lorry's dashboard (or is that a stereotype — do we see that a bit too often?). Perhaps he's actually wearing a suit – he's come from a funeral. Perhaps he's only got one arm, so that the protagonist feels bad about confronting a coal-man who's been humping sacks around one-handed. Perhaps we can have all three details. We expect someone driving a lorry to have personalised the cab and a teddy isn't uncommon, but we don't expect them to have one arm, or to be in a suit.

You can see we're beginning to get somewhere with this. Of course, as a writer, you might even fall a little in love with your coal-man, especially when you discover he isn't really a rip-off merchant, was always intending coming back with more coal and the funeral he'd just been to was his wife's.

But, backtracking slightly … the minor character as rip-off merchant has a long tradition. In *David Copperfield*, Dickens uses a scene from David's early life to show us how naïve his young hero is, as well as providing us with a bit of entertainment along the way. Copperfield, aged about eight, is alone in a Yarmouth coaching inn, waiting for the London coach. He is served up a meal by the waiter (who is, in fact, given the name William).

The waiter, under the guise of helping such a young boy bilks the lad out of most of his dinner and even wangles an over-large tip. Here's a little taste of the scene, where the waiter manages to get a free beer:

*After watching me into the second chop, he said 'There's half a pint of ale for you. Will you have it now?' I thanked him and said 'Yes.' Upon which he poured it out of a jug into a large tumbler, and held it up against the light, and made it look beautiful.*

*'My eye!' he said. 'It seems a good deal, don't it?'*

*'It does seem a good deal,' I answered with a smile. For it was quite delightful to me to find him so pleasant. He was a twinkling-eyed, pimple-faced man, with his hair standing upright all over his head; and as he stood with one arm akimbo, holding up the glass to the light with the other hand, he looked quite friendly.*

*'There was a gentleman here yesterday,' he said. 'A stout gentleman, by the name of Topsawyer — perhaps you know him?'*

*'No,' I said, 'I don't think-'*

*'In breeches and gaiters, broadbrimmed hat, grey coat, speckled choker,' said the waiter.*

*'No,' I said bashfully. 'I haven't the pleasure-'*

*'He came in here,' said the waiter, looking at the light through the tumbler, 'Ordered a glass of this ale — would order it — I told him not — drank it, and fell dead. It was too old for him. It oughtn't to be drawn; that's the fact.'*

*I was very much shocked to hear of this melancholy accident, and said I thought I had better have some water.*

*'Why you see,' said the waiter, still looking at the light through the tumbler, with one of his eyes shut up, 'our people don't like things being ordered and left. It offends 'em. But I'll drink it, if you like. I'm used to it, and use is everything. I don't think it'll hurt me, if I throw my head back, and take it off quick. Shall I?'*

*I replied that he would much oblige me by drinking it, if he thought he could do it safely, but by no means otherwise. When he did throw his head back, and take it off quick, I had a horrible fear, I confess, of seeing him meet the fate of the lamented Mr. Topsawyer, and fall lifeless on the carpet. But it didn't hurt him. On the contrary, I thought he seemed the fresher for it.*

Importantly, the story spreads amongst the other coach passengers that this young boy has eaten the most enormous meal and they give him some friendly teasing, so that when they stop for food, he goes hungry out of sheer embarrassment, despite the fact that he is starving as a result of William's con.

Dickens embeds plot points and our awareness of character by bringing in a minor player whom we quickly recognise, and I suspect the readers of Victorian Britain would have recognised even more readily. Indeed, there are a couple more waiter scenes as we see Copperfield mature and, eventually, become treated with a bit more deference.

If we're going to learn from The Greats, let's go to the top. Shakespeare too knew how to manipulate an audience by using minor characters. He was prepared to write scenes that would allow the audience to breathe a little, before moving onto the next big dramatic event. One of the best-known examples of this is in *Macbeth*.

Macbeth, egged on by his wife, has just killed Duncan, King of Scotland. Macduff, Macbeth's nemesis, arrives shortly afterwards. Shakespeare could let him find out about these deaths straight away, but he doesn't. The castle is firmly locked for the night. Someone has to let Macduff in, so instead of simply having some servant pull open the castle gate immediately, he both delays Macduff's entrance and has the incompetent, hard-of-hearing, half-cut porter come and do the job. The porter explains why it's taken so long to open the door by blaming it on drink.

*Porter: Faith, sir, we were carousing till the second cock; and drink, sir, is a great provoker of three things.*

*Macduff: What three things does drink especially provoke?*

*Porter: Marry, sir, nose-painting, sleep and urine. Lechery, sir, it provokes and unprovokes: it provokes the desire but it takes away the performance...*

The porter isn't just there for pure comic effect. What he tells Macduff is that everyone was very drunk and sleeping off the liquor. When Macduff finds Duncan dead, it is not unreasonable that no-one heard the killer. Indeed, as with our coal-man showing us that there's a coal-cellar, the comic relief here disguises the fact that the porter exists in a purely functional way to open a locked castle door and to explain why everyone has slept through a murder. You will read all sorts of literary analyses of how the porter scene echoes the concepts of knocking on the gates of Hell. That's all exceedingly clever and erudite, but from a writer's point-of-view, he exists because we need something to happen in the plot. A bit of relief from continuous tension means that the writer can tighten the screw again in a few minutes. A couple of simple plot points have been made much more enjoyable by wrapping them up in a fun character.

Variations on the deaf porter have become a staple of writers to this day. It's a technique you can employ time after time. And remember, the porter stays the same. He's a flat character. He doesn't change and suddenly spout, 'It's a miracle. After all these years I can hear again.'

Making minor characters quickly recognisable has several advantages. If they reappear, we know them instantly. As readers, if we don't have to work too hard on the minor players, then it means that we can concentrate on the principle characters in your book. As a writer, you know that once you've established some basic personality traits, then you don't need to dig further into the character. You don't need to decide what's going on in their heads or if their mothers treated them badly or if they take sugar or sweeteners in their tea.

Vitally, you're not shifting the focus away from the main story and the main characters by having us delve too deeply into the lives of people who are subsidiary to your story. And if you want to do that you can always have them re-appear in other novels or accept that the novel is now about someone else entirely.

## Over to you

Your character is in a hurry to get to an important event – a date, a crucial meeting, the bank vaults in time for the heist, their child's nativity play ... whatever. Concoct a short scene in which they are delayed, using a minor character to do it.

# 4

# Character actors and major stars

In the previous chapter, we looked at minor characters. We saw that either we had to make them entirely functional or could fatten them up with a few characteristics to make them a bit more interesting and hide a plot point or two. We could also use them to tell us something about our main character.

In this chapter, we're looking at the names in the credits that you recognise – the ones that get top billing. When they come to make the film of your book, these are the ones who will be in the frame when it comes to giving out the awards for best actor/actress or best supporting actor/actress. They are fuller, more rounded characters.

Obviously, you need to know far more about them than you do about your flatulent lift operator (the fact he's got flatulence is enough). As a consequence, you have to look beyond the surface detail that kept us happy when the waiter was nicking Copperfield's drink or the porter was cracking jokes about erectile dysfunction. If your walk-ons and minor characters are one-dimensional or two-dimensional at best, then this is where we need to be bulking out our creations, making them seem like genuine human beings.

True, there are plenty of books where the main characters are given no greater depth of characterisation than the coal-man, the deaf porter or the greedy waiter, but these are probably not the kinds of books that interest you unless you run short of fire-lighters. Otherwise it's unlikely you'd be reading a book on character creation.

For your main parts you want great, three-dimensional characters. What do we mean by that? Here is how James N. Frey describes them in his book *How to Write a Damn Good Novel*:

*They have complex motives and conflicting desires and are alive with passions and ambitions. They have committed great sins and have borne agonising sufferings; they are full of worries, woes and unresolved grievances. The reader has a strong sense that they existed long before the novel began, having lived rich and full lives. Readers desire intimacy with such characters because they are worth knowing.*

Our main characters need to be complex; we have to add layers to them. We have to make them more than the thumb-nail sketch of an officious parking attendant who wants £5 more because you've gone three minutes over the time.

Vitally, when writers talk about their main characters, they speak of them as if they were real, living, breathing people. How else can you make an imaginary person convince the reader unless you, the writer, feel as though one of your characters might at any point leap up from the page and drop in for a cup of tea, or seduce your husband or disembowel your favourite cat? According to Anthony Trollope (quoted in Miriam Allott's *Novelists on the Novel*), a reader cannot see characters unless the writer 'knows these fictitious persons himself, and he can never know them well unless he can live with them in the full reality of established intimacy'.

Our main characters can be (slightly falsely) divided into second- or first-level characters, so let's take a brief look at what we mean by these terms.

### Secondary rôles — character actors

In novels or stories, these are often the characters who will be the protagonist's friend or lover, rival or enemy. Into this category will fall villains, confidantes, father figures, characters who recur frequently throughout a book, with an important rôle to play in the plot's development. When they cast your film, these are the roles that will be filled by high-quality character actors, rather than the obvious leading man/leading lady type.

Second-level characters are extremely useful as a foil for your main character. Your protagonist needs a friend to speak to or an enemy to come up against. And these parts need fleshing out and making just as real as your first-level characters. Secondary characters are only secondary in the level of importance they play in your story. In terms of thinking about motivation, background and developing them into fully-fleshed human beings, they're just as important as your front-rank players.

## Quality not quantity

One of the traps it's easy to fall into is to create too many of them. We decide that the protagonist has two friends, but when we write these friends, we realise that they're not sufficiently differentiated. Do we actually need two people whose essential function is merely to comfort the protagonist or proffer advice or steal her boy-friend? Will one do?

Amalgamating characters can help you not only to reduce the number of people you're playing God with, but by joining up two sketchy characters that are under-developed, you can make a single, more fulfilling person who will come across more strongly to the reader. It's not a bad idea to stick to the rule that you need as few characters as possible to tell the story. Imagine you're making a film of your story and you have to pay out of your own pocket for every actor and extra you have in it.

## I think my second-level character should be playing the lead

Sometimes characters demand to take over a book. A minor character wants to be more than a bit player, a second-level character is much more interesting than the protagonist and has far more exciting problems to solve. What do you do if this happens and you suddenly find that your one-armed coal-man is the person you want to write about?

In her book *Bird by Bird*, Anne Lamott quotes Frederick

Buechner:

*If minor characters become major characters, as they're apt to do, you at least give them a shot at it, because in the world of fiction it may take many pages before you find out who the major characters really are, just as in the real world it may take you many years to find out that the stranger you talked to once for half an hour in the railroad station may have done more to point you to where your true homeland lies than your priest or your best friend or even your psychiatrist.*

According to Sebastian Faulks (*Faulks on Fiction*), Zoë Heller initially conceived of *Notes on a Scandal* without the character of Barbara Covett. Faulks describes this as like coming across a manuscript of *Hamlet* without the Prince himself in it. Highly-accomplished novels can be a long way down the line before the author actually realises which characters are important and which are not. Some bit-players, walk-ons and subsidiary characters can take over a book at a late stage in their development.

It is when the characters take over the writing of a story that a story is at its best. We have probably all seen soap operas in which characters, who, up until now have flapped around, suddenly change and become strong and directive, purely because the plot requires them to be that way. It's never entirely satisfactory when that happens. Go with the characters and see where they lead you.

## Major players

Often, a book or a story will have only one or perhaps two major players. In the rom-com, the heroine is likely to be the protagonist, but the love interest would fall into this first-level category. Likewise the detective's sidekick, if we see enough of him.

These are the characters that you have to ensure are going to thrill your reader. The major characters are the ones that we have

33

to know most completely as we write them. These are the characters we want to take flight as we write and to begin to act almost as though we are a conduit for their actions.

You can't know too much about these characters. However, you can tell your readers far more than they need to know. Whilst it may matter to you that your heroine has muesli for breakfast as that helps you to conjure up a picture of who she is, there's no point shoe-horning a breakfast scene into your book, just so that you can impart this vital piece of information to the reader.

They also have to be more than the sum of the story events that happen to them. John Braine gives us the following warning: 'You can, of course, invent only the details of character which you need for the purposes of the story. But in that case the characters will exist only for the purpose of the story. They won't move the story, the story will move them.' This brings us to the perennial writer's dilemma.

## Major characters and plot

Which comes first: character or plot? This is the chicken-egg conundrum of all writers.

Before we go any further, let's define what we mean by the word 'plot'. Writers tend to use the words 'plot' and 'story' more-or-less interchangeably, which must annoy anyone who has had the difference between the terms drilled into them in formal English literature classes.

E. M. Forster famously defined the difference between the two as:

*'The king died and then the queen died' is a story. 'The king died, then the queen died of grief' is a plot.*

In other words, the actual events of a narrative are story. The mechanics of what happens, why one situation arises directly out of another, is the plot. A corpse is found, the police have to investigate. A woman discovers her husband's adultery, which leads to a divorce.

The novelist Linda Anderson, in the book *Creative Writing*, gives us a nugget of great advice:

*It is a good idea to envisage character and plot as interlocking, rather than starting with a plot idea and then adding in characters. See how events emerge naturally from character.*

The modern taste is for work to be character-driven rather than have characters do whatever is dictated by the strictures and structure of the plot. This hasn't always been the case.

Aristotle's *Poetics* is often thought to be the first set of writings on dramatic theory/literary criticism. It can also be seen as a kind of primer for writers, especially of Tragedy. His work dates from the 4th Century BC. Literature and poetry were vital to the intellectual life of Ancient Greece. Even today, writers pay attention to what he has to say — it's famously used by Hollywood scriptwriters, although you may not necessarily think that this is a recommendation. In *Poetics*, Aristotle creates a hierarchy of importance for the elements of drama. He chooses plot, which he describes in my translation as the 'soul of tragedy', as being the first principle of drama. Character comes second. This is then followed by dialogue, form of words, then 'the spectacle'.

Aristotle was also a biologist and he had a huge desire to classify what he saw. Whilst much of what he has to say is still relevant, I would suggest that we're living in different times. Ideally we want character and plot so interwoven, so interlocking that neither can be changed without huge knock-on effects for the story we're telling.

In Forster's king-and-queen plot, we only have the sketchiest of outlines for what might become a story or a novel, yet already we know something about the characters involved. They are obviously aristocratic — you can't get much further up the social scale than the monarchy. We also know that the queen loved her husband so much that she was unable to live without him.

If you were going to write this story, you have free rein to do a lot of things with these characters. Are the king and queen really a king and queen, or have they been overthrown by republicans and are living out their lives in exile? Do they like the ceremony and the pomp, or are they more at home wearing jeans and trainers? Does the queen love the king because he is kind and loving, or despite the fact that he is haughty? How old are they? How did the king die? Was it suicide, old age, assassination, cancer or a bungee-jumping accident?

Forster's 'plot' can also be regarded as an over-arching story arc in its own right. Indeed, we might be better off putting the term plot to one side and calling what we have here the 'situation' or the 'set-up'. If you've ever dipped into a film guide or read the listings, you'll know the kind of thing I mean:

My elderly copy of *Haliwell's Film Guide* summarises one film (based on a novel) thus:

*A man-eating shark causes havoc off the Long Island coast.*

Yes, of course, it's *Jaws*. This one-line summary gives us a basic set-up. If we were to write this idea from scratch, we still need to people it with real characters, decide who is going to chase the shark, who is going to want to keep the beaches open, where our conflict is going to lie.

Coming at an idea from a basic story set-up is an excellent way of creating both story and characters. Many writers arrive at the ingredients of their stories using this method. Indeed, a television programme on Scottish crime writer Ian Rankin saw him take a newspaper headline concerning a man who drove up and down a major road looking for his missing daughter and begin shaping this basic situation into a novel. Rankin keeps various cuttings in a folder and when time comes for him to start his next book, he looks at the kinds of stories that might interest him.

John Braine also says something similar, '... it's impossible to determine whether the story emerges from the characters or the characters from the story.' Somehow, moving around the potential ingredients of a story will allow both the actual mechanics of the plot and the characters to emerge.

We can do the same thing.

We pick up a news-in-brief item about a Death Row inmate and decide it would be something we might like to write about.

Let's imagine that our main character, the one awaiting the chair or the needle, is trying to prove his innocence. Perhaps we like the idea of drawing the reader in, to believe the main character's innocence, only to have him released and commit another murder. Or perhaps we could have him condemned, only to have the same kind of crime committed again — obviously by somebody else. Anyway, whichever way we do it, we want to toy with the reader and then pull the rug from beneath them, because that's the mood we're in today. We feel compelled to write this story, but we're not sure how to go about it. It all hinges on that central character.

We can make our Death Row inmate a witty, charming, artic-ulate, middle-class man or we can make him a slow-witted fall-guy. We can make him a she. If we make the character a well-spoken, articulate accountant, then how he has ended up on Death Row is likely to be very different from the ratty, small-time drugs dealer trying to pay for his own habit. We then start throwing into the mix all sorts of possible ideas. Is he going to try to prove his own innocence, or does he have a lawyer or a prison visitor who could try to do this? If we go with the prison visitor, could we maybe choose a woman who has been writing to Death Row inmates? And if she has been doing this, why? Is she some kind of perverse groupie, or doing so from religious conviction or does she think that a relationship with a man behind bars is the only kind she can have? Or does he have a decent pension, and if he agrees to marry her, she'll get half after his death?

You can see already that as we start nibbling at the potential elements of the story, we can't help but think about the characters. What we're hoping for is that the characters will begin to force the plot to fall into place. This is how the late John Mortimer, whose most famous creation is the gluttonous barrister Rumpole, worked:

*... as a character begins to talk, or comes into conflict with another, the plot may start working; because it's important that the characters perform the plot and the plot doesn't manipulate the characters...The moment when the characters take charge is one of great happiness for the writer.* (From Clare Boylan, *The Agony and the Ego*.)

Besides, a character can't occur in a vacuum. Captain Ahab's hatred for the big white whale would be entirely theoretical if all he did was sit at home and mope about it. His obsession drives the plot of *Moby Dick*. Yes, you could create a character who is obsessed with something other than a whale, but then every choice they made would then drive the plot. Someone obsessed with making ships in bottles in his garden shed? Have the Council come along with a demolition order. Oops, a lot of those missing school-children seem to be underneath it ...

As Nancy Huddleston (quoted by Janet Burroway and Elizabeth Stuckey-French in *Writing Fiction*) says,

*Because character and event are interlocked, stories don't end in accident; rather the consequences of the story come from the character who determines events. Our decisions make us who we are forever afterwards.*

So we're going to look at a variety of ways of drawing on the world around us to further our ability to create interesting characters. But our main characters, the stories they engender, the milieu in which they live — all these must interlock if we are to grab and maintain the reader's interest.

## Over to you

Find a tiny snippet from a newspaper, such as a headline, or a news-in-brief item. Don't investigate the story any further, but use the brief outline to think of how you might people the story. Here are some headlines to get you started. You may prefer to find your own, of course:

- Anti-social crimes on rise in town
- Villagers to buy closed pub
- Mayor pledges to tackle parking issue
- Man tries to open aircraft door mid-Atlantic
- Woman charged after threat to nurses
- Hang-glider pilot hurt in crash
- Newts moved ahead of railway work

# 5

# What can we steal? Using real people

There's a village called Ry, a dozen miles or so from Rouen in Upper Normandy. Walk down its main street of half-timbered buildings and you'll see signs declaring 'Le Bovary', 'Galerie Bovary', 'Emma' and 'Le Flaubert'. There's also a Bovary Museum, where Emma Bovary's tragic, implosive story is bizarrely re-told using little automata. There's a statue of Flaubert in the car-park. If you haven't got the message yet, yes you're in *Madame Bovary* territory.

The reason for all these references to Flaubert's most famous character can be found at the 12th Century church. Its biggest attraction should be the intricate, carved renaissance porch. But it isn't. In the graveyard is a plaque, which reads 'To the memory of Delphine Delamare, née Couturier, Madame Bovary, 1822-1848'. For this is where the aforementioned Delphine Delamare was buried.

Poor Delphine was the unhappy wife of a local doctor. In order to cheer herself up and escape the reality of small-town, parochial Ry, she had a stream of lovers, but in the end decided that the only way out of her humdrum existence was by swallowing poison.

It does sound remarkably like the plot of *Madame Bovary*. But where the idea that Delphine was the inspiration for Emma has come from, I haven't been able to establish. Of course, this story would have been all over the local press in mid-19th Century Normandy and Flaubert must have heard of it and there's a reference to a Madame Delamare in a letter to Flaubert from a friend. However, the notion that Delphine must without doubt be the model for Emma Bovary certainly gains traction when you see that graveyard plaque has been erected by the National

Federation of the Writers of France. Surely they must know.

Besides, the English translator of the Penguin Edition of Madame Bovary, Geoffrey Wall, goes along with the Delphine-as-Emma theory in his biography of Flaubert, although he also adds two other women into the mix. He reckons that Emma is a composite of Delphine, Louise Pradier, a promiscuous socialite who (like Emma) ran up huge debts, and Flaubert's sister Caroline who died in childbed. Given he's an expert, that seems reasonable enough. Yet, in Miriam Allott's book Novelists on the Novel, Flaubert is reported to have said:

*When I'd finished Madame Bovary I was asked several times 'Was it Madame XXX whom you intended to portray?' And I received several letters from perfect strangers, one of them from a gentleman in Rheims who congratulated me on having avenged him! (for a faithless woman). All the chemists in the Seine-Inférieure recognised themselves in Homais and wanted to come and slap me in the face; but best of all (I discovered this five years later) at that time in Africa an army doctor's wife called Madame Bovaries who resembled Madame Bovary, a name which I'd invented by altering Bouvaret.*

Using real lives as the basis for fiction has a long and glorious past. Alexander Selkirk is often supposed to be the inspiration for the character of Robinson Crusoe in the first novel written in English. Even today, writers still dip into other people's lives as a resource. Why? Well, for some reason, we like the idea that characters are based on real people. When we hear that the notorious serial killer Ed Gein is supposedly the inspiration for Thomas Harris's Hannibal Lecter or the Buffalo Bill killer, Jame Gumb, it gives the reader an added frisson of realism.

Ed Gein gets about a bit, too. He is also supposed to be the basis of the Norman Bates character in *Psycho*. Whether it is true or not is difficult to know. Besides, being 'the basis' doesn't mean to say that you have to use the entire life story of that person.

Indeed, Thomas Harris's Buffalo Bill also uses the same ploy as another real-life serial killer, Ted Bundy, to lure women into his van. He wears his arm in a cast and asks for help shifting a piece of furniture. One suspects that whilst researching ideas for the book, Harris must have read up a great deal on serial killing. If you're going to write the character of a serial killer, you're going to end up with a mishmash of bits based on reality as well as adding in some of your own ideas.

Indeed, using bits and pieces is a common technique. One of the difficulties of simply lifting lives wholesale is that lives are haphazard, whereas fiction tends to be a neater version of real life. If you merely re-write a life in such a fashion that it sounds like fiction, you run the risk of losing impetus in your story. Our lives don't tend to have neat narrative arcs. Often the weakest stories I'm given to read are ones where the writer says 'well, it's what really happened.' You also need to bear in mind that fact is genuinely stranger than fiction, which tends to sew things up a bit more neatly. You couldn't invent a character such as Harold Shipman, because no-one would believe that a fictional doctor could possibly kill that many victims and get away with it for so long without anyone in authority noticing. Similarly, coincidences that occur in real life sit badly in works of fiction – we always find them too contrived, unless, of course, it's a Thomas Hardy novel, then we let him get away with it.

Some authors are more deliberate in picking over the bones of real life than others. W. Somerset Maugham spent a good deal of his life collecting stories and characters from his travels, especially in the Far East. In the end, he had to keep on moving from one ex-patriot circle to the next. He was probably collecting yet more material, but it also must have saved him from being beaten up too often. Dickens went very close to the mark on some of his characters. He even wrote to a certain Mr. Haines asking for a favour about a London magistrate:

*In my next number of Oliver Twist I must have a magistrate; and casting about for a magistrate whose harshness and insolence would render him a fit subject to be shown up, I have as a necessary consequence stumbled upon Mr. Laing of Hatton-garden celebrity. I know the man's character perfectly well; but as it would be necessary to describe his personal appearance also, I ought to have seen him, which (fortunately or unfortunately as the case may be) I have never done. In this dilemma it occurred to me that perhaps I might under your auspices be smuggled into the Hatton-garden office for a few moments some morning.*

The Allan Stuart Laing who features in this letter was well-known for the nastiness and severity of the punishments he meted out. Dickens was committed to social reform and saw part of his rôle as a writer to point out these kinds of injustices. However, writing a character who can so easily be identified is not always the wisest of choices and British libel laws (of which more later) are draconian, illogical and in need of reform.

You can't, however, libel the dead, so you could use someone who is no longer with us, so long as you don't stray into the territory of accidentally including their friends and relatives who are still living and defame them instead. If you're drawn to writing historical novels, or even stories set in the near-past, then there's a fine tradition of fictionalising people from history's pages. At the time of writing, Hilary Mantel has enjoyed enormous critical and commercial success with books based around Thomas Cromwell, who rose from nowhere to become adviser to King Henry VIII. Jane Seymour, King Henry, Thomas Cranmer and Anne Boleyn are amongst the various real, but long-dead, characters Mantel brings to life.

She's not alone. There are examples of these from all across fiction by some of our finest authors. Peter Carey created a fictionalised version of Ned Kelly for *True History of the Kelly Gang*. Robert Graves dug into the Roman Empire for many of his books, including *I, Claudius*, and into the Victorian justice system for *They Hanged my Saintly Billy*. Michael Cunningham's *The Hours*, with its three time strands, has a fictionalised version of the novelist Virginia Woolf as a main player. Julian Barnes dips into the story of the wrongly-gaoled George Edalji, the victim of Dreyfus-like racial prejudice, whose case was picked up by Arthur Conan Doyle and turned into a cause célèbre, and uses the two men to create *Arthur and George*. Shakespeare did it all the time.

## Grand theft autobiography

Trawling history is one thing; using your own life another. Of course, there are some novels that are thin disguises of the author's own experiences. Céline's *Journey to the End of the Night*, Lawrence Durrell's *Alexandria Quartet*, Sylvia Plath's *The Bell Jar* and Marcel Proust's entire output are all examples of works that are based to some extent on the authors' own lives. Charles Bukowski's low-life stories are based on his years of heavy drinking in urban California.

Others focus on their own social circle. Neal Cassady is the model for Jack Kerouac's Dean Moriarty in On the Road. Carlos Fuentes's *Diana: The Goddess Who Hunts Alone* is essentially a portrait of the American actress Jean Seberg, with whom he had an affair whilst she was still married to Romain Gary, who in turn used her as a character in his own book *White Dog*.

I once read a biography of Bukowski and it felt as if I'd heard all the stories before, because they were retellings of various events in his life that appear in his stories and novels. The cynic (or at least the sceptic) might ask the question, 'So why didn't they just write a straight autobiography/memoir?'

I can't answer that question, save by reiterating that this is just one place from where writers draw their characters. Perhaps some people are drawn to fictionalising their own lives, because for them that makes what they write more realistic. On the other hand, you can normally tell that when a novelist starts having novelists as their main characters, they probably should be getting out more.

Some of the pitfalls and difficulties of re-writing your own life are pointed out by Raymond Carver in a *Paris Review* interview:

*Of course you have to know what you're doing when you turn your life's stories into fiction. You have to be immensely daring, very skilled and imaginative and willing to tell everything on yourself. You're told time and time again when you're young to write about what you know, and what do you know better than your own secrets? But unless you're a special kind of writer, and a very talented one, it's dangerous to try and write volume after volume on The Story of My Life... a little autobiography and a lot of imagination are best.*

In other words, if you are going to use your life as a resource, move your ideas on, using it only as a starting-point. The unpleasant scene where you were begging the bank manager unsuccessfully for a loan can always emerge as the triumphant way in which your heroine funds the first of what is going to be a chain of megastores.

## Thinking like an actor

There is one hugely important way in which you can draw on your own life, however, and that is borrowing a trick used by actors. It's not easy for an actor to cry, laugh, show fear or excitement at will. Actors often delve into their own past and use their emotional response to an experience to recreate that emotion on the stage or the screen.

As an example, you may want to write a scene set in a crowded restaurant in which our heroine is told by her nasty lover that he doesn't love her and he never has. This may never have happened to you, but you have to get all the hurt and humiliation your heroine is feeling onto the page. Scrolling

through the film of your own life, you try to find an occasion when you felt hurt and humiliated. What might that be? When you fell at the second hurdle on school sports day with hundreds of people watching? You felt pretty small then, combine that with an occasion when a boyfriend gave you the old heave-ho and, despite the fact he did it with tact and consideration, you were upset and surprised. Now you're moving towards feeling what your heroine feels. Sometimes you have to dig deep to get what you need.

Flaubert is famously reputed to have said, 'Madame Bovary, c'est moi!' Although at first glance, it's hard to imagine that a chubby, syphilitic male could masquerade as a bored housewife with delusions of grandeur, there's an element of truth in the statement. We know from all his writings that Flaubert was bored by his surroundings and carried on an affair with the married poet Louise Collet for several years. Using bits of real life is not the same as using life in its entirety.

For every one of the examples of a book based on a real person, there are hundreds that are created from myriad sources. All of our characters are bound to have something of our own lives in them. This might be our own direct experience, or filched, either subconsciously or deliberately, from all those little newspaper stories and overheard snippets on trains and buses and from people we meet.

Writers pick inside themselves for different aspects of their personality to create characters. True, the non-writing public likes to think that writers take people from real life, but the reality is, as Margaret Atwood says, that they 'steal the shiny bits'. The trick is to spot those shiny bits.

## Libel and other offences – a caveat

If you lift someone from life and drop them into a novel or real life, you run the risk of upsetting them, if not actually defaming them.

A small town in the Midlands was up-in-arms a while back when residents thought they could see themselves in various portraits of village life in a self-published e-book. Whilst the idea that villagers were fictionalised in its e-pages gave the author plenty of publicity, even hitting some of the big daily newspapers, the poor on-line reviews would suggest that, rightly or wrongly, some locals were upset.

You could argue that at least it got reviewed and some publicity, but offending the neighbours (which I very much doubt the author intended) is a dangerous way to drum up interest in the press. And if someone did decide you'd libelled them, then you could be on dangerous ground.

Libel law is a hugely complex area and the libel laws can change at any moment. In England and Wales at least, they are also bizarre and punitive, with the emphasis being placed on the defendant to prove that he or she didn't libel the plaintiff. But the main aspect that you need to think about is if people are likely to recognise themselves, then you should either come up with an entirely new character or disguise the person so completely that they are unrecognisable. Changing gender, place of work, age, dress and so forth should make a real person no longer able to spot themselves. But then again, if you do that, then why not invent your character from scratch?

If you think for any moment that you stand a chance of defaming someone, then don't. Just changing the name doesn't work. Libel can occur when you thinly disguise your unpleasant boss, George Schultz, by calling him George Schmidt. However, be cautious about this too. You can libel people accidentally. If you decide to call your inept surgeon, who staggers from one botched operation to another, Fiona McLeish, only to find that there is indeed a real surgeon called Fiona McLeish, she could also sue you. Check the medical register!

If we return to Flaubert's explanation of how he developed the character of Emma Bovary for a moment, it could be that what he said about creating the character was, in fact, a lie in order to save the feelings of those left behind in the wake of Madame Delamare's suicide and to avoid a costly court case.

## Over to you

Think about someone you know – someone with a big personality. Rule a sheet of paper (or two) down the middle. Down the left-hand side, make a list (in no matter what order) of what you know about them. Using the character checklist might help you here. Now, go through the list and against anything you've got on it that could even remotely identify the person in question, change the information and jot it down on the right-hand side. If the person is a man, make her a woman. If they live in Kent, move them to Aberdeen, if they like keeping fit, make them sedentary, if they are generous, make them tight-fisted – and so on. Once you have changed as much as you can, read down your right-hand list. Do you have the outline of a possible character?

# 6

# What can we steal? Types, archetypes, stereotypes

One of my relatives works for an international company. She reckons that national stereotypes exist at least in part because they are true. When she phones the German subsidiary, whatever task needed doing will have been done. 'Of course, we did that last week, immediately when you asked. Anyway, you said you would be telephoning at 10 o'clock. I was expecting your phone call then. Already it is 10.15.' When she gets in touch with the subsidiary in Spain: 'We haven't quite got round to that, yet, because ... well, we have so much to do, you know. We will be doing it, soon. Tomorrow, maybe.'

The difficulty with stereotyping is that whilst a touch of it may make an amusing anecdote, in anything more substantial, you're delivering something a bit too obvious to the reader. With racial stereotyping, you're on exceedingly thin ice. It's a matter that's dealt with by Art Spiegelman in his graphic narrative *Maus*, which tells his father's life as a Jew in Nazi-occupied Europe. In the book, Spiegelman moves between visiting his father's house many years after the war and his father's war-time story in the death camps. Spiegelman Sr. is awkward, tight-fisted and demanding. In one point in the frame narrative, Spiegelman Jr. complains to his step-mother, 'It's something that worries me about the book I'm doing on him. In some ways he's just like the racist caricature of the miserly old Jew.'

Spiegelman is dealing with a real person. He's trying to be honest and true-to-life in his portrayal, but even so, he is worried that he's writing a stereotype. The French may not be the international champions at brainstorming (*Mais, c'est pas possible!*), but they certainly don't spend their lives cycling round wearing striped jerseys and berets with a string of onions round their necks. Yes, if you want a cartoon Frenchman for a third-rate comedy sketch or in a pantomime, the stripy cycling onion may sneak through. But it's not very useful if you want your characters to have resonance.

In life, we often 'type' people very quickly. We're doing it every time we look at our fellow-passengers on a train. *She's a bit scruffy. Does he have to shout into the phone? I hope she doesn't come and sit next to me.* We especially do it with other road-users. *Why can't the Nissan Micra driver not get above 40 mph? Isn't it about time Audis were equipped with indicators? Does a tartan rug on the parcel shelf mean you're forced by law to pull out at junctions without looking?*

However, whilst we may not want to spend a huge amount of time in the company of a character who is obviously a stereotype, these characters do have their uses, as we've already seen when discussing walk-on and minor parts.

In some ways, there is nothing new under the sun. Many of the archetypes we come across in modern forms of literature and drama have evolved from traditional tales and early varieties of street theatre.

From fairy tales, we have such stock characters as the wicked stepmother, the fairy godmother, the innocent child, the old hag or the older man – such as a king – who has little idea of what is happening around him. All these still exist in slightly different shapes in modern literature. We just have to be a little bit more inventive as our readers and audiences become more sophisticated. Let's dip back in time, though, to see how characters were handled down the centuries.

## Theophrastus and *The Characters*

A pupil of Plato and Aristotle, Theophrastus was a Greek polymath who made a life's work out of attempting to categorise the world around him. He wrote several works on physics, metaphysics and, perhaps most famously, botany. In amongst all this, in around 300 BC, he penned a series of thirty character sketches (although some doubt its authenticity).

All his types are still recognisable today, proving that for all we get smarter and buy cleverer gadgets, deep down we're all capable of greed, vanity and a touch of unenlightened self-interest. Despite the fact that Theophrastus claimed he was setting down both the good and the bad traits of human beings, the emphasis seems to be on the less pleasant side of human nature, although his descriptions are seamed through with acidic humour.

Edmonds's 1929 translation of the work gives us the following categories of behaviour, to which I've added a few notes in brackets to clarify one or two terms that seem a bit old-fashioned or are used slightly differently now:

1    Dissembling (being two-faced)
2    Flattery
3    Garrulity
4    Boorishness
5    Self-seeking affability (pretends to be good-natured to get own way)
6    Wilful disreputableness (a scallywag)
7    Loquacity (incontinence of speech)
8    News-making (the gossip)
9    Unconscionableness (doing anything for money, shameless)
10   Penuriousness (tight-fistedness)
11   Buffoonery
12   Tactlessness
13   Officiousness
14   Stupidity
15   Surliness
16   Superstitiousness

17   Querulousness (the grumbler)
18   Distrustfulness (assuming everyone is dishonest)
19   Nastiness
20   Ill-breeding
21   Petty pride (displays of wealth)
22   Parsimony
23   Pretentiousness
24   Arrogance
25   Cowardice
26   Oligarchy (desires power)
27   Opsimathy or Late-learning (second childhood, no I'd never heard of opsimathy either)
28   Backbiting
29   Friendship with Rascals
30   Meanness (To be honest, I can't see a great deal of difference between this and Nos. 10 and 22)

Recognize patterns of behaviour in that lot? There's enough stupidity (No. 14) around to keep the sellers of flimsy celebrity-obsessed magazines in business and reality TV programmes on our small screens. What are rock groups who indulge in high-profile hotel-room wrecking other than wilfully disreputable (No. 6)? Behave this badly and you're bound to be in the papers. What are international power-brokers with bizarre hairstyles, trophy wives and billion-dollar portfolios other than desirous of power (oligarchy, No. 26)? Say one word against this type of person and they will set in motion the might of their expensive legal team to stop your mouth, pen and keyboard forever.

Theophrastus is great fun. It's almost as if you can order characteristics as if they were items on a take-away menu.

Some of Theophrastus's descriptions are absolute gems. Take this snippet from his elucidation of ill-breeding (No. 20):

*When he is eating with you he will relate how he once took hellebore and was purged at both ends, and the bile from his bowels 'was as black as this soup'.*

Yes, we've all sat round the dinner table and listened to inappropriate discussions of the wrong end of the alimentary canal. Similarly in his description of meanness (No. 30), Theophrastus says, according to another translation I found on the wicked world-wide web of wonder:

*Entertaining his clansmen, he will beg a dish from the common table for his own servants; and will register the half-radishes left over from the repast, in order that the attendants may not get them. Again, when he travels with acquaintances, he will make use of their servants, but will let his own slave out for hire; nor will he place the proceeds to the common account. It is just like him, too, when a club-dinner is held at his house, to secrete some of the fire-wood, lentils, vinegar, salt, and lamp-oil placed at his disposal. If a friend, or a friend's daughter, is to be married, he will go abroad a little while before, in order to avoid giving a wedding present.*

I suspect we've all got a couple of friends like this. They may not have slaves or servants, but they never turn up with a bottle of wine and if you go out for the day, it's always your petrol that gets used.

There's plenty still to be learned from Theophrastus and translating his pre-Christian archetypes into their modern day equivalents might certainly give you a useful minor character, or if developed more fully, perhaps even a major character.

## Commedia dell' Arte,

Moving across the centuries and slightly round the Mediterranean, we come to Fifteenth Century Italy and Commedia dell' Arte. This was a little like an early form of pantomime where set characters, identified by the masks they wore, improvised routines. If that sounds a bit like *The Fast Show*, *Little Britain*, the consistent casting of types in the *Carry On* films or indeed any sketch show with recurrent characters, then it's hardly surprising, because they're essentially just modern-day counterparts.

The Commedia dell'Arte's characters were based on types which, like those of Theophrastus, still resonate down the years. The characters were divided into three groups – the lovers (Innamorati), the servants (Zanni) and the masters (Vecchi).

The masters all held positions of power and/or wealth. Of course, comedy allows us to pick on people like that – there's only the cruellest of humour to be had in kicking people who are already down. However, pricking the pompous and the self-important is always good for a laugh. The silent comedies of Charles Chaplin, Harold Lloyd and Buster Keaton replicate elements of Commedia dell'Arte. The Marx Brothers' routines could almost have been lifted entirely from this form of pantomime, although they arrived at their routines without ever having heard of this kind of theatre.

There's not the space here to go into all the characters, but a quick glance at a few will quickly show that essential character-istics (and plots) endure.

Il Capitano (the Captain) was a caricature of a military gentleman, who whilst he swaggered around boasting of his exploits would hide behind the ladies' skirts the moment there was a whiff of any trouble. A direct descendant of his can be seen in the Duke of Plaza-Toro from Gilbert and Sullivan's Operetta *The Gondoliers*. The chorus sing of him, 'In enterprise of martial kind, when there was any fighting, he led his regiment from behind — he found it less exciting.' In less comic circum-stances, modern-day dictators have a tremendous capacity for covering their shoulders in gold braid and filling their chests with medals.

Similarly, Pantalone would be based on the idea of a rich

Venetian merchant who had made piles of money and there was no way he was ever going to part with any of it. He often had a younger wife or a headstrong daughter he needed to keep in check. Stern patricians keeping their eye on the wilful females of the family is a staple to this day. Indeed, it is essentially the character of General Sternwood in Raymond Chandler's *The Big Sleep* and of Lear in Shakespeare's *King Lear*. Both of these are serious versions of this stock character, whereas Baron Hardup in *Cinderella* would be a direct comedy descendant.

Amongst the servants, Columbina was the straight part. She was a female servant, who tended to be cleverer than anyone else involved in the pantomime. You can see her in more up-to-date form in the character of Polly in *Fawlty Towers*, who is the voice of reason and intelligence, when everyone else around her is demonstrating incompetence. Brighella, another of the servant class, was a bit of a rogue, always on the look-out to make money. How different is he from Del Boy in *Only Fools and Horses* or Sergeant Bilko of *The Phil Silvers Show* (or *Top Cat*, its feline cartoon equivalent)?

The comedies of Molière and Shakespeare both owe a lot to the Commedia dell'Arte. Indeed, if you were to read through a blue-print of Commedia dell'Arte, with its sets of lovers, masters and servants, it looks like an outline sketch for *A Midsummer Night's Dream*.

## Archetypes and fairy tales

It's not unreasonable to describe all of these stock characters as archetypes, especially as we can see their direct descendants in action to this day. Archetypes are to be found in all sorts of works for the stage, screen or page. They arise from all the traditions that we've just examined. According to my dictionary, an archetype is 'an original pattern or model'. In his book *The Writer's Journey*, which analyses how popular films work, relating them to characters and plots from traditional mythology,

Christopher Vogler, describes archetypes thus:

*As soon as you enter the world of fairy tales and myths, you become aware of recurring character types and relationships: questing heroes, heralds who call them to adventure, wise old men and women who give them magical gifts, threshold guardians who seem to block their way, shape-shifting fellow-travellers who confuse and dazzle them, tricksters who upset the status quo and provide comic relief. In describing these common character types, symbols and relationships, the Swiss psychologist Carl G. Jung employed the term archetypes, meaning ancient patterns of personality that are the shared heritage of the human race.*

Vogler goes on to point out that archetypes are part of the universal language of story-telling and that they are 'amazingly constant throughout all times and cultures'. Note also that Vogler refers to character types and not stereotypes. What Vogler suggests is that an archetype has a plot function within a story. According to Vogler, we have rôles such as the hero, the mentor, the herald, the threshold guardian and the trickster.

The hero or heroine is the protagonist of our story, the person we're going to have to root for. Traditionally, we experience the story through the hero's eyes. We expect them to be made wiser and more mature by their adventures. In Vogler's myth, the questing hero has to go in search of the Elixir. This is their plot function. James Bond, with his ready repartee, his fast cars and bedroom banter is a questing hero. But so too is the aspergic Christopher Boone of *The Curious Incident of the Dog in the Night-time*. As characters, they could barely be less alike. Christopher is dogmatic, inflexible and unworldly. Bond is quick-witted, adaptable and knowing. But both are on quests. Bond needs to defeat SMERSH; Christopher needs to find out who killed the dog.

Help and hindrance to the hero/heroine's quest comes at him

in various guises, including that of the mentor or wise old man/woman. Often, our hero/ine needs someone from whom to take advice. The advice also often comes from some older figure – in *Star Wars*, the Alec Guinness character gives Luke pointers on how to wield a light sabre. In the French film, *Bienvenue Chez Les Ch'tis (Welcome to the Sticks)*, the idea of a mentor is parodied, when the central character is going to be posted from the warmer climes of the Bouches-du-Rhône to the north of France and takes advice from his wife's great uncle about how to survive living in such a potentially cold and inhospitable climate.

Similarly, we need obstacles to the protagonist's progress. The threshold guardian, for instance, has to test our hero or heroine in some way. Often, in mythology, they will set a riddle or a task that our protagonist has to solve or answer before moving onto the next level of their adventure. In real life, a threshold guardian would be a burly gentleman in an ill-fitting dinner suit whose catch phrase would be 'No trainers!' However, any book will have a series of threshold guardians, if we interpret the archetype in a broader sense. At any twist or turn of the plot, our protagonist must suffer setbacks: the detective is sent on a dead-end chase by the false confession; the girl is told by her father that he doesn't want her meeting the boy. These are (although perhaps not strictly by Vogler's definition) instances where our protagonist is set back by the deeds of someone else.

We've seen from our discussion earlier of major and minor characters and by paddling in the shallow end of older forms of story-telling that sometimes there really is nothing new under the sun. Types, archetypes, stereotypes exist both in the real world and in literature. Your job as a writer is to bring something interesting to these types to raise them above the level of stereo-typing and breathe new life into them, so that the reader can enjoy a fresh, new character.

## Over to you

Write a brief character sketch, based on one of Theophrastus's categories. If you feel ambitious, write one humorous sketch and one in a more serious vein.

# 7

# What can we steal? Birth signs and bumps

Celtic astrology doesn't divide us into star signs, but classifies us into trees, according to the dates of our birth. Apparently, I am an ash.

A quick visit to the Forestry Commission's website tells me I should therefore have compound leaves with slightly toothed edges, distinctive black winter buds and a smooth grey bark with more fissures as I get older.

Celtic astrologers, on the other hand, have a completely different view of me. They would have me be marked by sense of ambition rather than my foliage. Amongst the good things that they have to say about me are that I am uncommonly attractive (not just attractive, but uncommonly so), intelligent and talented. Amongst the less flattering of my attributes are that I am egotistical and impulsive and like to play with fate. If I were a cedar tree, on the other hand, I'd be of rare beauty, which is even better than being merely uncommonly attractive. Oh, how the fates of the midwives, castor oil, gas and air, and the epidural can change our lives. But then again, if I were a cedar tree, everyone would have to put up with the fact I would be impatient and look down on people.

There are many astrological systems (can using trees actually be astrological? Surely it would have to be dendrological or something) in addition to the Western tradition we tend to read in our daily newspaper. According to that fount of all knowledge, Wikipedia, you can have a choice of at least the following: Celtic, Hindu, Chinese, Korean, Vietnamese, Greek, Roman, Egyptian, Ancient Islamic, Babylonian, Mayan, Tibetan, Burmese as well as our Western version.

Read any description of any astrological sign and you're

bound to find a bit of yourself in them. More importantly, they can be used as a cue for working out characters. It doesn't matter which you plump for. You don't have to believe in the stars (or your trees) to make use of them in your imaginary worlds. In fact, it's possibly far better if you don't, as you won't get hung up thinking 'Oh, an Aries would never do something like that.'

Importantly, the various signs can be adapted to help us create people for our fictional worlds. If you look up what astrologers make of people born under the star sign of Gemini, you may see something along the lines of 'dual personality, charming, witty, life and soul of the party, but you can be seen as shallow ...' And if we scope out the sign of Virgo, we might find that we come across someone whose weaknesses might be that they are 'fussy, interfering and inflexible'.

To me, as an agnostic in matters astrological, it would seem that we have a built-in baseline of conflict between two characters with such different characteristics. So if we simply put a Gemini in an office with a Virgo and see how they get on, then we've actually got the vaguest of notions for a plot — a situation or set-up. Importantly, it's a plot based on character.

Let's make our skittish Gemini bored with the workplace. He's going to liven it up by bringing in doughnuts, singing at his desk and sending fake emails from the company hierarchy, telling people that it's come to their attention that the cacti are being over-watered, they're using too much company sugar in their coffee or that they must wear colour-coded clothing according to the day of the week. Meanwhile, the Virgo is busy trying to alphabetize the filing system, make sure that everyone uses their own mug and, every Monday, she brings in an expensive little bagless vacuum-cleaner to do the bits of her cubicle the cleaning staff missed. She also likes to get in a bit of tooth-sucking and tut-tutting whilst doing it. The Gemini, of course, finds this inter-ruption to his canny bidding on an on-line auction annoying. When Virgo pops out for lunch, Gemini likes to open up the vacuum cleaner and put in the little plastic toys she has lined up so neatly along the little shelf in her cubicle. Whenever she notices they've gone and then spots them in the Perspex dirt collector, she goes mad. She knows who's done it, but can't point the finger of blame at her colleague, because she has no proof.

Here, we've already got the basic ingredients of a light comedy drama. After all, a fuss-pot and a joker aren't necessarily going to rub along. But we can ramp up the stakes. What happens when there's a promotion in the air? What happens if they both fancy the new job, but, of course, only one can get it? What happens if one of them will have to be made redundant, but both joined at the same time and the management can't make up their minds who should go?

Look at any horoscope or star sign and you have the raw ingredients for potential characters. And I do mean 'raw ingredients'. They can be nothing more than a starting point.

By checking out the sign of Leo, I find that some of that character's attributes are that they are confident, ambitious, generous, loyal and encouraging. We could then make a nice, warm character based on these aspects of personality. Of course, we need to know so much more, but we have the vaguest of rough outlines of how such a person faces life.

On the other hand, we could look at Leo's weaknesses and choose from vanity, pretentiousness, the need to be domineering, propensity for melodrama or their stubbornness. Mix these together and, again, you've got quite a different personality emerging. Start picking from the list of strengths and weaknesses, and you're creating something more complex again.

Whilst none of this is sufficient for a full character, it has the advantage that at least it can start your thoughts moving. It provides a well into which you can dip your bucket.

## Feel your bumps for further inspiration

Phrenology is another area you can ram-raid for ideas for what might make characters tick. For some reason, whilst some other pseudosciences are alive and kicking, despite overwhelming evidence that they are pure hokum, phrenology is in a bit of a slump period. That's a bit of a shame, as those replica phrenology skulls are pretty nifty and would look just the business on a writer's shelf.

I suspect the reasons for its decline might come from the racist intentions to which it was put from time to time, but there's no need for any of that nastiness with what we're about to do.

According to phrenology, the actual shape of the skull determines various aspects of your personality, so a fully-trained phrenologist can run his refined, educated fingers through the luxuriant growth on your head and tell a great deal about you. Different areas of the brain, apparently, create different propensities, sentiments and intellectual and reflective capacities. The undulations, the little dips, valleys and rises of the human skull can tell us what lies beneath. This is because, contrary to what we have discovered from genuine anatomy and physiology, the brain has 26 organs that affect the shape of the skull.

Early on in the development of phrenology, its practitioners believed that amongst these organs, there were specific theft organs and murder organs. Unfortunately, these ideas fell by the wayside as phrenologists aimed for greater 'accuracy' and developed a list of what they called 'propensities'. If you look at the phrenologists' categories of propensity, there are various basic ideas that can be explored. Phrenological propensities include:

- Cautiousness
- Secretiveness
- Acquisitiveness
- Conscientiousness
- Wit or mirthfulness

Any of these could be used as a basis for a character. If we make a character cautious, for instance, we can then think about what scenarios to put him in. What kind of cautiousness could that be — financial, physical, when driving? What about cautiousness of ambition? She'd like a new job with fresh challenges, but the pay's OK and she's used to the people she works with and if she changes, she may not like it. Or perhaps, we could try cautiousness in love? He's once bitten, twice shy, but all his friends are beginning to get paired up, so they are anxious that he shouldn't be on his own and insist on introducing him to a series of entirely inappropriate mates.

Of all the propensities dreamed up by the phrenologists, my personal favourite is philoprogenitiveness, which is apparently the desire to have lots of children. Our philoprogenitive hero could be a bed-hopping cad or the world's most kindly *pater familias*. On the other hand, we could make him the sole male survivor in some post-apocalyptic dystopian story. Forced to mate with all the women of the island to keep the human race going, he could either have a whale of a time, or we could make him gay, and thus his life would be one of eternal misery. Of course, philoprogenitiveness is not the preserve of men. After all, the old lady who lived in a shoe of nursery rhyme fame obviously had this propensity. We could have a heroine, whom we could either make ridiculously fecund, or sadly infertile. In fact, we could do anything we wanted as all we're doing is using the seed of a characteristic to start trying to grow characters and story ideas in tandem.

There are plenty of belief systems about our nature on which you can draw for the basic outlines of characters. But it is only when you start to move beyond the basics, that you will begin to get genuine flesh-and-blood characters emerging.

And, by the way, if you think all this Celtic astrology stuff is nonsense, my wife is a fig tree, which means that amongst other things she does not allow contradictions or arguments. How wrong I was to be so sceptical?

## Over to you

Find a straightforward description of one of the signs of the Zodiac, e.g. what is a typical Aries or Sagittarius. Then get hold of a horoscope - it doesn't have to be for the same star sign. You'll find that the horoscope will often be vague: you have big decisions to make, someone in your life will let you down, you are in for a bit of good fortune for a change. Using the vague outline of the horoscope and that of the personality, see if you can concoct a story in which your character acts according to the characteristics set down in the star-sign summary. If you browse the Internet, you'll find all sort of useful potential starting points where astrologers labour their ideas on character further under such headings as 'Capricorn in love', 'Leo in love', 'Making friends with a Scorpio'.

# 8

# What can we steal? Learning from psychologists and psychopaths

Every few years, the American Psychiatric Association publishes a large manual, *The Diagnostic and Statistical Manual of Mental Health Disorders* (*DSM*) for the guidance of psychiatric doctors and nurses.

The book is controversial in that some critics argue that it medicalises what are essentially basic human traits, although there is not the space to go into that here.

Nor do I want to trivialise genuine mental health problems, but there are certain areas of human behaviour that the manual flags up that are useful as starting points for a writer's journey into character.

To give you a flavour of what is in the handbook, here are some of the disorders and conditions that might help trigger more character-cum-story ideas:

- Age-related cognitive decline
- Alcohol abuse/dependence
- Alzheimer's disease
- Amnesia
- Antisocial personality disorder
- Anxiety disorder
- Attention deficit disorder
- Bereavement
- Bibliomania
- Binge eating disorder
- Body dysmorphic disorder
- Caffeine-related disorder (indeed, find me a writer who hasn't got this)

- Circadian rhythm sleep disorder
- Claustrophobia
- Communication disorder
- Conduct disorder
- Depressive disorder
- Eating disorders
- Erotomania
- Frotteurism
- Generalized anxiety disorder
- Hypochondriasis
- Impulse control disorder
- Inhalant abuse
- Insomnia
- Kleptomania
- Male erectile disorder
- Mathematics disorder
- Mood episode
- Morbid jealousy
- Narcissistic personality disorder
- Neglect of child
- Night eating syndrome
- Obsessive-compulsive disorder
- Oppositional defiant disorder
- Panic disorder
- Partner relational problem
- Pathological gambling
- Persecutory delusion
- Premature ejaculation
- Pyromania
- Reading disorder
- Sadomasochism
- Selective mutism
- Shared psychotic disorder (what used to be called *folie à deux*)

- Sleep terror disorder
- Sleepwalking disorder
- Substance-related disorder

There's a whole host of other conditions, but hopefully, you'll agree that's there's plenty of potential material here, although as with all these basic traits, and ideas taken from astrology, Theophrastus, the Commedia dell' Arte or phrenology, they need scoping out and expanding. If you stick too close to the source idea, you risk writing stereotypes or clichés.

Bizarrely, there are also certain topics that take off from time to time and magazine editors are suddenly inundated with stories on that theme. One short-story competition judge recently told me that she'd had a whole raft of Alzheimer's stories in one contest. Similarly, when I taught creative writing for the Open University, I would often find that certain themes, for no apparent reason, seemed to be the topic of the year when it came to final assessment. There's obviously something in the air.

It is sheer bad luck to hit on a set of characters who are dealing with a problem that is suddenly topical. But I also think that if you push at you subject matter, making your characters as interesting as they possibly can be, then they can seem fresh and subject matter that may seem to have been used often before can suddenly take on a new complexion.

For each of the disorders listed above, all of us are somewhere on the bell curve. Most of us get depressed from time to time, but few of us get so depressed that we become unable to get out of bed or become suicidal. We don't have to use each disorder to its maximum in order to help us create characters. Let's take Social Anxiety Disorder as an example.

The vast majority of us will feel some kind of social anxiety in certain situations. If you're going to have to give a talk or a business presentation or represent the company you work for at some event, you are almost bound to feel some level of tension.

You may be fine talking with people face-to-face, but not particularly enjoy speaking on the telephone as you can't see the other person's face, and thus their reactions. The vast majority of us feel some level of anxiety in different social situations.

Outside that vast majority, at one extreme of our graph are the people who thrive on this kind of situation, who are not thrown at all by it. They may be brash, opinionated, downright stupid, socially inept and unaware or have been brilliantly trained for it at their expensive school. At the other end, some people live in abject terror of very ordinary social situations. There are people so shy, that if asked a question they might run away and lock themselves in the nearest lavatory. There are people who are so worried by the thought of other people watching them eat, that they could never venture into a café or restaurant or take up an invitation to dinner.

Now, you may not want your character either to be so brash that the average reader would want to club him to death or so terrified of social situations that they daren't venture out of the house. It may be that your character is at neither extreme, but for the sake of the story, you have her give a presentation at a conference. How anxious are you going to make her? Not a twinge of anxiety? A touch of nerves? Physically sick, but able to do it eventually? Lying on the floor of her hotel bedroom, screaming?

We can take any of these topics and explore them. For example, if we use as our starting-point bibliomania, a condition not unknown amongst writers, then what could we do to create characters for a short story?

I don't know about you, but I'm allergic to that aimless recreational shopping whereby you drift from one store to the next examining everything on display without knowing what you're going to buy. I pillory people whose wardrobes are full of clothes bought on such expeditions, yet never worn, or bought a size too small in some vain hope that their purchaser would shed half a stone before the wedding/birthday/Christmas/first Sunday after Trinity. Yet stick me in a book shop and I'll browse for hours on end, picking up a stack of books, and, yes, some go unread.

So could we create a warring couple? One of them is bookish, will only spend money on intellectual pursuits, the other is drawn to fashion and the bright surfaces of things. Maybe that's too obvious. Does it have to be books? Surely any obsession would do. Can we have a character who spends all the time in his shed — doing what? Making bird-tables or nesting boxes, or scale models or ships in bottles, or commanding miniature soldiers at the Battle of Waterloo? Start to worry away at the idea of an obsession and we can quickly move from one idea (someone who buys too many books) to someone determined that he will beat the local war-gaming champion, even at the risk of cheating and keeping a spare General von Blücher in his pocket in case of emergencies.

Obsessional behaviour pushes characters to extremes and another extreme of character can be found amongst the psychopaths who tread our streets.

## The Hare Psychopathy Checklist

I first came the notion that there might be a way of testing for psychopathy in Jon Ronson's clever and funny *The Psychopath Test*. Ronson trained to use the Psychopathy Checklist (Hare PCL-R), developed by Professor Robert Hare. He then used it to interview various subjects to discover whether or not they were psychopaths. Of course, immersed in the world of the psychopath, Ronson then finds himself judging all sorts of people he encounters in daily life, weighing up if they might be psychopaths, rather than just unpleasant.

Of course, as with any set of personality traits, as we've already seen, all of us have them to some degree or other. For instance, one of the signs of psychopathy is having a glib and superficial manner. Surely many of us, thrust into a social situation against our will, have put on a front and been both glib and superficial. It doesn't mean we want world domination, though.

The Hare checklist is another handy device for thinking about characters. You can apply it to much more than just your villains, though. These are the traits that are assessed:

- Behavioural problems in childhood
- Callousness and lack of empathy
- Criminal versatility
- Cunning and manipulativeness
- Failure to accept responsibility for own actions
- Glib and superficial charm
- Grandiose, over-exaggerated estimation of self
- Impulsivity
- Irresponsibility
- Juvenile delinquency
- Lack of realistic long-term goals
- Lack of remorse or guilt
- Many short-term marital relationships
- Need for stimulation
- Parasitic lifestyle
- Pathological lying
- Poor behavioural controls
- Revocation of conditional release (they get sent back to gaol for breaking terms of parole)
- Sexual promiscuity
- Shallow affect – in other words, any emotional response is entirely superficial

Again, if we pick any one of these traits, we can begin to use it as the basis of a character. If we look at the idea of parasitical lifestyle, for instance, we could create a range of possible characters, including:

A young adult who can't be bothered to find a job, because it's far easier living off Mum and Dad than it is actually finding a job. Perhaps the young adult moves from one course to the next, failing at everything, but constantly being bailed out by indulgent parents. Perhaps a bit too obvious.

An entire family with no work ethic at all. To avoid cliché, we won't make them live on a tough estate, but we'll make them apparently well-off and house them in something the size of a rectory and give them a private income. If we gave them private means, perhaps it's not quite enough to enable them to live in the manner to which they aspire, so they're the kind of people who don't return dinner invitations, never stand a round of drinks, recycle presents by unwrapping them very carefully and then relabeling as appropriate. 'If you don't want that, I can make good use of it ...'

## The Enneagram of Personality

In addition to tests, such as the Hare-PCL-R, there are various other personality-types questionnaires that have different reputations, according to whichever source you read. We're not worried here about their validity as genuine scientific tools, but are interested in how useful they can be as a starting-point for any character-cum-story-situation we might care to develop.

Amongst these tests is The Enneagram of Personality. The enneagram gives us nine basic personality types, and in addition gives us four traits for each personality type:

- The reformer (principled, purposeful, self-controlled, perfectionist)
- The helper (generous, demonstrative, people-pleasing, possessive)
- The achiever (adaptable, excelling, driven, image-conscious)
- The individualist (expressive, dramatic, self-absorbed,

temperamental)
- The investigator (perceptive, innovative, secretive, isolated)
- The loyalist (engaging, responsible, anxious, suspicious)
- The enthusiast (spontaneous, versatile, acquisitive, scattered [no, I'm not sure what they mean by that either — perhaps flits from one thing to the next?])
- The challenger (self-confident, decisive, wilful, confrontational)
- The peacemaker (receptive, reassuring, complacent, resigned [to what, we're not told])

If we treat these in the same way as we looked at archetypes, we can see that the personality types of the enneagram are recurrent figures in literature and movies. At a straightforward level, what is the 'peacemaker' other than the sheriff riding into town to clean the place up? Every boxing movie has a 'challenger'. What is 'the investigator' if not the detective, hot on the trail of the killer? The detective can be anything from the unlikely little old lady on a black utility bicycle, to the entirely unlikeable sodden lout, but the notion of 'the investigator' gives us this immediate idea. Your investigator doesn't need to be investigating a murder either. The wronged lover is going to try to find out who is cuckolding them. They may enlist a friend ('the helper') to see if they can discover what is going on. Isn't 'the reformer' just about every other character played by Jimmy Stewart?

There is a host of other personality tests. We're not worried about their scientific reliability, but how useful they are for raiding for ideas for character creation. Amongst the tests you might take a look at are:

- Personality and Preference Inventory
- Myers Briggs Type Indicator
- Minnesota Multiphasic Personality Inventory

- Big Five Personality Traits (Openness to experience, conscientiousness, agreeableness, extraversion, neuroticism)
- Raymond Cattell's 16 Personality Factors

## Over to You

Pick one of the disorders from the DSM. Alternatively, take a look at the American Psychology Association website for a condition. Begin sketching out a character who might have one of these traits. Try to think beyond the obvious stereotype. Then take that character and put them in the worst possible situation they could be in and see how they react. For example, if you have someone who is unable to eat in public, make them sit at the top table in a formal setting, where they are the focus of attention, such as a bride at a wedding breakfast might have to endure.

# 9

# Introducing a character

## More than just a pretty face

When we watch a film, we have the huge advantage of having the physical description of any character done for us by the camera. If we've got a knock-kneed beggar, we can see them there on the screen. There's no reason for us to think long and hard about how much we need to describe either the knocking of the knees or the begging. The actor, together with the costume department, director and so forth will conjure up the character for us.

Physical description is always a difficult one to call. How much does the reader want to know about what someone looks like before the character actually does anything and moves the plot on? Indeed, how much does the reader want to know about what a character looks like at all? Does the reader need to know about height, hair or eye colour, weight and build? Perhaps they do. Only you can decide and only you can decide how you're going to get this information across to the reader. Are you going to go for a front-loaded description, or drop in little dollops as the story unfolds? Indeed, are you going to do any physical description at all?

Until quite recently, it was standard practice to find set-pieces describing physical characteristics of every character as they were introduced. Even minor characters would get a paragraph or two before opening their mouths. But even if we look at a couple of examples from writers who, by modern standards, seem quite wordy, then it's interesting to note that they don't always linger over the physical descriptions of even their most important characters.

Thomas Hardy is famed for writing lengthy descriptive passages. The scrubland of Egdon Heath gets about seventeen pages at the start of *The Return of the Native*, which is enough to make the most patient modern reader reach for the smelling salts to stay awake. Even the prolix Hardy manages to keep his visual description of his most famous heroine down to a few lines. Our first encounter with Tess Durbeyfield gives us only this in the way of description:

*A young member of the band turned her head at the exclamation. She was a fine and handsome girl – not handsomer than some others, possibly – but her mobile peony mouth and large innocent eyes added eloquence to colour and shape. She wore a red ribbon in her hair, and was the only one of the whole company who could boast of such an adornment.*

We have to wait several paragraphs whilst her father embarrasses her in front of her friends, before Hardy gives us a bit more of her, telling us about her way of speaking, which gives him another chance to focus on her physical features:

*The pouted-up deep red mouth ... had hardly as yet settled into its definite shape, and her lower lip had a way of thrusting the middle of her top one upward, when they closed together after a word.*

*Phases of her childhood lurked in her aspect still. As she walked along to-day, for all her bouncing handsome womanliness, you could sometimes see her twelfth year in her cheeks, or her ninth year sparkling from her eye; and even her fifth would flit over the curves of her mouth now and then.*

*...A small minority, mainly strangers, would look long at her in casually passing by, and grow momentarily fascinated by her freshness, and wonder if they would ever see her again: but to almost everybody she was a fine and picturesque country girl, and no more.*

Importantly, Hardy has got movement into this description – a point we will pick up on again in a later chapter. Tess turns her head; we see the shape of her mouth when she speaks. By avoiding static description, he makes her alive.

George Eliot's introduction of Dorothea Brooke in *Middlemarch* combines a physical description with Dorothea's general attitude to life:

*Miss Brooke had that kind of beauty which seems to be thrown into relief by poor dress. Her hand and wrist were so finely formed that she could wear sleeves not less bare of style than those in which the Blessed Virgin appeared to Italian painters; and her profile as well as her stature and bearing seemed to gain the more dignity from her plain garments, which by the side of provincial fashion gave her the impressiveness of a fine quotation from the Bible, or from one of our elder poets, in a paragraph of to-day's newspaper. She was usually spoken of as being remarkably clever, but with the addition that her sister Celia had more common-sense ...* [several lines later]...

*Young women of such birth, living in a quiet country-house, and attending a village church hardly larger than a parlour, naturally regarded frippery as the ambition of a huckster's daughter. Then there was well-bred economy, which in those days made show in dress the first item to be deducted from, when any margin was required for expenses more distinctive of rank. Such reasons would have been enough to account for plain dress, quite apart from religious feeling; but in Miss Brooke's case, religion alone would have determined it; and Celia mildly acquiesced in all her sister's sentiments, only infusing them with that common-sense which is able to accept momentous doctrines without any eccentric agitation.*

Eliot is an absolute mistress of interweaving appearance and attitude. Yes, the sentences are a tad lengthy for modern taste, but we soon have a pen portrait of Dorothea, her uncle and her sister. It takes around eight pages for Eliot to establish these three characters before we start the action. *Middlemarch* is a large-cast book, which appeared in chunky instalments, so ensuring the characters are firmly established in the reader's mind makes sense.

You will still find more contemporary writers who give us a description of the protagonist before unleashing them on the world. It can be a very effective method. John Kennedy Toole's protagonist Ignatius Reilly from the book *A Confederacy of Dunces*, is also introduced as a mix of both physical and attitudinal description in this way:

*A green hunting cap squeezed the top of the fleshy balloon of a head. The green earflaps, full of large ears and uncut hair and the fine bristles that grew in the ears themselves, stuck out on either side like turn signals indicating two directions at once. Full, pursed lips protruded beneath the bushy black moustache and, at their corners, sank into little folds filled with disapproval and potato chip crumbs. In the shadow under the green visor of the cap Ignatius P. Reilly's supercilious blue and yellow eyes looked down upon the other people waiting under the clock at the D. H. Holmes department store, studying the crowd of people for signs of bad taste in dress. Several of the outfits, Ignatius noticed, were new enough and expensive enough to be properly considered offences against taste and decency. Possession of anything new or expensive only reflected a person's lack of theology and geometry; it could even cast doubts upon one's soul.*

*Ignatius himself was dressed comfortably and sensibly. The hunting cap prevented head colds. The voluminous tweed trousers were durable and permitted unusually free locomotion. Their pleats and nooks contained pockets of warm, stale air that soothed Ignatius. The plaid flannel shirt made a jacket unnecessary while the muffler guarded exposed Reilly skin between earflap and collar. The outfit was acceptable by any theological and geometrical standards, however abstruse, and suggested a rich inner life.*

Ignatius dresses so outlandishly, that he is an obviously comic character. If you passed him in the street, you'd at least take a second look. I suspect you might even be tempted to film him on your camera-phone and have him on the Internet by the time you got home. But Ignatius doesn't just dress this way because he has no dress sense, he actually does have coherent reasons for turning out like an accident in a charity shop. He wants to avoid catching cold, so his cap has little ear-flaps, and likes his trousers loose so he can walk comfortably. Vitally, we also get something of his worldview, which seems as bizarre as his dress sense. Why should theology and geometry matter when we're looking at the way people dress?

Ignatius is, of course, a larger-than-life figure. The entire book is the story of Ignatius's eccentric battle against the world, so describing him up-front makes sense. We need to be able to stand with him, so that despite all his bizarre short-comings (and he has many), we still manage somehow or other to be on his side. Indeed, Ignatius is one of the great comic creations.

## Physical description as focus

Physical description can also make the reader realise who is important within a scene as Flaubert shows in his opening to *Madame Bovary*, when we meet poor Charles for the first time:

*We were in class when the head-master came in followed by a 'new fellow', not wearing the school uniform, and a school servant carrying a large desk. Those who had been asleep woke up, and everyone rose as if just surprised at his work*

*The headmaster made a sign to us to sit down. Then, turning to the form-master, he said to him in a low voice, 'Monsieur Roger, here is a pupil whom I recommend to your care; he'll be in the second class. If his work and conduct are satisfactory, he will go into one of the upper classes, as becomes his age.'*

*The 'new fellow', standing in the corner behind the door so that he could hardly be seen, was a country lad of about fifteen, and taller than any of us. His hair was cut square on his forehead like a village chorister's. He looked reliable, but very ill at ease. Although he was not broad-shouldered, his short school jacket of green cloth with black buttons must have been tight around the arm-holes, and showed at the opening of the cuffs red wrists accustomed to being bare. His legs, in blue stockings, looked out from beneath yellow trousers, drawn tight by braces. He wore stout, ill-cleaned, hob-nailed boots.*

Importantly, Flaubert doesn't describe the headmaster, the school servant or Monsieur Roger. This is because they have no great part to play here. The important character is the 'new fellow'. And whilst we get a fairly static description of him, if you were to read the whole opening chapter, you would see that this is actually interspersed with bursts of action in which, for instance, we see Charles being teased over his hat, his way of pronouncing his own name and watch him as he does his homework, looking up every word in the dictionary.

A further point of interest about Flaubert's description of Bovary is that he points out the kinds of things that other schoolboys would notice. For instance, there's no mention of hair or eye colour – unless these were radically different why would another boy care? No, we see the things that anyone would at first glance. Later, as we see more of Charles Bovary, we get to see other things too, but Flaubert gives us enough of both the situation and Bovary's physical characteristics to give us the picture.

## Character-in-action

Elvis Costello's song *Satellite* starts with the line, 'She looked like she'd learned to dance from a series of still pictures.' It could almost be a blue-print for writing sharp, accurate description. We may not know what this woman looks like, but we do know how she dances. Apparently, Alan Plater's character notes for the character of Trevor Chaplin (played by James Bolam) in The Beiderbecke Affair read, 'Trevor always walks as if it's raining.'

This too is in keeping with the modern taste for description, which is to have pithy words and phrases that do a huge job, whilst seeing the character in action.

Nowadays, we usually see characters already doing something, rather than have a big physical-cum-attitudinal build up, with what we know about them being inferred by the reader. The modern reader has a massive visual vocabulary, culled from pictures, films, television and the net. We are used to processing information extraordinarily quickly. In the main, we want to get on with the action, whatever that action might be. Staying put as we take a still picture of our character, before we allow ourselves the luxury of animating them and having them actually do something, can be a bit tedious.

Setting the characters off, then having the reader discover things about them as they go along is probably a much better way of ensuring that readers are hooked in. They want to read on to discover more about the characters, who reveal themselves in snippets as the novel unfolds. Michael Martone is quoted in Janet Burroway's *Writing Fiction*, 'As you read, the details fall like snow that suddenly is ash. The character is clearly visible once he is coated, like a statue in the town square after such a storm, with a film of detail.' It sounds much more intriguing than winding up characters like clockwork mice before letting them loose on the reader.

Yet, there are hugely successful books that break this mould altogether. In novels such as Brown's *The Da Vinci Code* and Larsson's *The Girl with the Dragon Tattoo*, we often learn vast amounts about a character as s/he is introduced, before that character actually begins to do anything to move the story along. This is more-or-less what film scriptwriters do as anyone reading the script pre-production needs to have an image of who might play that part.

## Let's see their worldview

When we introduce a character, we can also give something of their view on the world. We can see that Ignatius is complex, eccentric, probably lacks self-awareness and is possibly self-centred, just from the snippet above. We can also get the story moving along, even as we introduce a character.

One of the great introductions of 20th Century literature that combines physical description and the character's attitude whilst moving the story along has to be Raymond Chandler's opening to *The Big Sleep*. Chandler's detective, Philip Marlowe, tells the story in the first person:

*It was about eleven o'clock in the morning, mid-October, with the sun not shining and a look of hard wet rain in the clearness of the foothills. I was wearing my powder blue suit, with dark blue shirt, tie and display handkerchief, black brogues, black wool socks with dark blue clocks on them. I was neat, clean, shaved and sober, and I didn't care who knew it. I was everything the well-dressed private detective ought to be. I was calling on four million dollars.*

*The main hallway of the Sternwood place was two storeys high. Over the entrance doors, which would have let in a troop of Indian elephants, there was a broad stained-glass panel showing a knight in dark armour rescuing a lady who was tied to a tree and didn't have any clothes on but some very long and convenient hair. The knight had pushed the visor of his helmet back to be sociable, and he was fiddling with the knots on the ropes that tied the lady to the tree and not getting anywhere. I stood there and thought that if I lived in the house, I would sooner or later have to climb up there and help him. He didn't seem to be really trying.*

*There were French doors at the back of the hall, beyond them a wide sweep of emerald grass to a white garage, in front of which a slim dark young chauffeur in shiny black leggings was dusting a maroon Packard convertible. Beyond the garage were some decorative trees trimmed as carefully as poodle dogs. Beyond them a large greenhouse with a domed roof. Then more trees and beyond everything the solid, uneven, comfortable line of the foothills.*

Marlowe is established straight away. The description of his clothes shows us that not only is he a man for detail, but the implication is that he's smartened himself up for the job. As with Ignatius, we have a reason for the clothes he's wearing.

He's sharp-witted (*I was sober and didn't care who knew it*). And the description of the luxury he encounters is both witty and shows us that this isn't his natural milieu. Even the joke about the stained-glass window is a clever indicator that Marlowe is capable of rescuing someone. It's either some deliberate foreshadowing by the author (can Marlowe rescue a damsel in distress?) or if not, then it's a neat coincidence that can give the literary critics something to write about for decades to come.

And, vitally, the story has got underway: Marlowe has been called to the Sternwood mansion. From his cynical world-weary description of it (and how smartly he dresses to go there), we know that this wealthy world is alien to him. We also know that he's about to be given a case to investigate. *I was everything the well-dressed private detective ought to be.*

Importantly, the tone of the entire book is set by the descriptions of Ignatius and Marlowe and, perhaps to a lesser extent, that of Dorothea.

## Telling us about a character before we meet them

It's also worth bearing in mind that we can use what others say before we meet a character. This allows the reader to build up a picture of them, so we feel as though we know them by the time they arrive on the scene. In *The Great Gatsby*, Scott Fitzgerald uses this to great effect as party-goers at one of Jay Gatsby's lavish affairs — weekend parties with plenty of illicit alcohol during America's prohibition era — speculate about their host:

'I like to come,' Lucille said. 'I never care what I do, so I always have a good time. When I was here last I tore my gown on a chair, and he asked me my name and address — inside of a week I got a package from Croirier's with a new evening gown in it.'

'Did you keep it?' asked Jordan.

'Sure I did. I was going to wear it tonight, but it was too big in the bust and had to be altered. It was gas blue with lavender beads. Two hundred and sixty-five dollars.'

'There's something funny about a fellow that'll do things like that,' said the other girl eagerly. 'He doesn't want any trouble with **anybody**.'

'Who doesn't?' I enquired.

'Gatsby. Somebody told me —'

The two girls leaned together confidentially.

'Somebody told me they thought he killed a man once.'

A thrill passed over all of us. The three Mr. Mumbles bent forward and listened eagerly.

'I don't think it's so much **that**,' argued Lucille sceptically; 'it's more that he was a German spy during the war.'

One of the men nodded in confirmation.

'I heard that from a man who knew all about him, grew up with him in Germany,' he assured us positively.

'Oh no,' said the first girl, 'it couldn't be that, because he was in the American army during the war.' As our incredulity switched back to her she leaned forward with enthusiasm. 'You look at him sometimes when he thinks nobody's looking at him. I'll bet he killed a man.'

All this speculation, as well as making us realise that Gatsby is the kind of man people just have to talk about: he's intriguing, the rumours are flying, we don't know how he made his money. What little they know about him — his generosity and his wealth — gives rise to all the gossip. This means that by the time we meet him, Gatsby is intriguing to us as the reader as well. As it happens, he doesn't appear until Chapter 3. In my paperback copy, he finally makes his entrance on page 53 of a book that runs to only 188 pages.

This is also a technique that is used with villains, of which more later, when we start getting more villainous.

## Over to you

Write a scene in which a character is introduced before she or he actually enters the scene. For instance:

- Three friends are due to meet for a meal or a drink or coffee. Two of them arrive at the allotted hour and start discussing the third, who is late.
- A speaker on the platform at an international conference is given a big build-up by the person chairing the event.
- A possible employer skims through a candidate's CV just before interviewing them.
- A lonely man receives emails from a woman he's met on the Internet, before going to meet her in person.

# 10

# Character in action – why showing is better than telling

It is always far more effective if we see a character in action rather than relying on the narrator to tell us things about him or her. Doling out information doesn't pull the reader into your fictional world. At a simple level, if you've got a tall character, rather than telling us they're tall, have them stoop as they go through a doorway. Got a character with no dress sense? Let's watch them decide what to wear for that all-important big date or for a smart job interview. Got a nervous character? Have them chew a pen-top or their nails, or laugh at anything anyone says. We should always be trying to write a cinema film, rather than a still picture.

We've seen something of this in the previous chapter where we discussed ways of introducing a character. And here's another example — Larry Weller in action from the opening of Carol Shields' book *Larry's Party*.

*By mistake Larry Weller took someone else's Harris Tweed jacket instead of his own, and it wasn't till he jammed his hand in the pocket that he knew something was wrong.*

*His hand was travelling straight into a silky void. His five fingers pushed down, looking for the balled-up Kleenex from his own familiar worn-out pocket, the nickels and the dimes, the ticket receipts from all the movies he and Dorrie had been seeing lately. Also those hard little bits of lint, like meteor grit, that never seem to lose themselves once they've worked into the seams.*

*This pocket – today's pocket – was different. Clean, a slippery valley. The stitches he touched at the bottom weren't his stitches. His fingertips glided now on a sweet little sea of lining. He grabbed for the buttons. Leather, the real thing. And something else – the sleeves were a good half inch longer than they should have been.*

The whole of this extract involves action, with only the tiniest snippets of static information (e.g. *the sleeves were a good half-inch longer*). From this, we learn (or at least infer) at least the following:

- Larry Weller has probably just been in some kind of public place — a café or a restaurant perhaps?
- He must be a bit absent-minded. He's picked up the wrong jacket and should have been able to tell from the length of the sleeves.
- His pockets are normally crammed with stuff that should be chucked away. He's probably a bit unkempt. Maybe a bit of a hoarder back home.
- He seems to go to the cinema a lot — perhaps he lives in a city, so he's got a wide choice of films.
- He goes to the cinema with Dorrie? Is she a girl-friend or a wife? Somehow, we expect a wife. Do people with tweed jackets have wives rather than girl-friends?
- Harris Tweed. What does that signify? It surely makes him older, or from a different era. Perhaps the story is set in the recent past. Is it maybe the kind of jacket a college professor would wear?

His jacket is likely to have cost less than the one he took. His doesn't have the leather buttons. Either he's not that well-off, or he doesn't care enough to spend the extra on better buttons. Besides, you get the impression that his buttons would get unthreaded and fall off before he ever noticed.

It could be so easy to write a static version:

*Larry Weller was the kind of guy who would accidentally pick up the wrong jacket. And he wouldn't even notice until he put his hand in the pocket and found that it wasn't full of the usual junk — old tissues, bits of lint, cinema tickets.*

*Larry liked the cinema and he and Dorrie had been going a lot recently...*

But with Shields' version, we get so much more. She makes him come alive, because we see him in action. Action also has the benefit of automatically adding in the magic ingredient of movement. Shields uses words, especially verbs, that imply movement (*jammed, travelling, pushed down, balled-up, worked, touched, glided, grabbed*). This technique lifts this description onto an entirely different plane from my static version and we enter Larry's world.

Entering the character's world is vital. We feel what is going on vicariously when a skilled writer gives us a character in action. For instance, in Kingsley Amis's novel *Lucky Jim*, Jim Dixon wakes up after a night of heavy drinking in someone else's house:

*Dixon was alive again. Consciousness was upon him before he could get out of the way; not for him the slow, gracious wandering from the halls of sleep, but a summary, forcible ejection. He lay sprawled, too wicked to move, spewed up like a broken spider-crab on the tarry shingle of the morning. The light did him harm, but not as much as looking at things did; he resolved, having done it once, never to move his eyeballs again. A dusty thudding in his head made the scene before him beat like a pulse. His mouth had been used as a latrine by some small creature of the night, and then as its mausoleum. During the night, too, he'd somehow been on a cross-country run and then been expertly beaten up by the secret police. He felt bad.*

Amis could simply tell us that Jim drank too much and has a bad head the next day, but by showing Jim dealing with the aftermath of his drinking (he also discovers that he's dropped a cigarette on the bedclothes), we get right inside the character's head, and share the way it throbs with him.

Applying that mantra of 'show, don't tell' makes us animate characters in a way that we simply can't by doling out pure information. So let's imagine for a moment that we want to show that someone is confused. Of course, we could write something, such as:

*Jean looked confused for a moment.*

There's nothing wrong with that if the confusion isn't particularly important, but if we want to genuinely mess with a character's emotions and get the reader feeling what a character feels, then we need to think what their actual reaction to a confusing situation might be.

What kinds of behaviour do people exhibit when they are confused?

They might look round to see if anyone else can help explain, knit their eye-brows together, screw up their face, not finish their sentences or stammer when replying, tug on an ear-lobe or scratch their forehead. They may also begin to perspire a little more than normal, although probably not as much as they would do if frightened or simply hot.

Outward signs can obviously be interpreted in several different ways. Knitting your eye-brows might simply mean that you're concentrating. Similarly, if you chew your lip, you could be thinking, or it might be a nervous habit, or it could simply be that you've got something stuck on it. But if we give a scene a little context and the character a couple of these little traits, then the reader is going to understand the situation and we allow ourselves the luxury of dropping in bits of information, as Shields does with the length of Larry's sleeves, that don't feel lumpen and awkward. You've also involved your readers by having them deduce the character's emotional state from the clues in the text, rather than telling them outright. Reading is a two-way process and if you tell your reader too much, they're not contributing and will switch off.

*'Standard deviation is an extremely basic statistical tool and one that is easy to grasp,' said Mr. Thomas.*

*Jean stared at the problem in front of her. It was all just numbers — a meaningless jumble of figures. Perhaps she should have just stuck with English lit. She looked over the desk at Rob and raised her eyebrows.*

You get the idea.

Having a character **do** something, rather than **be** something shows us how they behave. It also has the added benefit of moving your story along. Pause too long for us to take stock of a character and we can go off the boil.

When we talk about 'action', we don't necessarily mean big set-piece action. We don't necessarily mean gun-fire, explosions, kidnapped heiresses or bronzed limbs intertwining as the bed breaks beneath thrashing bodies. Even the most minor actions can have a resonance as we saw with Larry's mistaken jacket or Jim's over-indulgence.

Let's take another example. We want an office cleaner as a character in a story. What kind of cleaner do we want? We could have someone who likes cleaning, someone who hates cleaning; someone who is careful and proud of their work or someone who is cavalier.

If your office cleaner carefully moves everything to one side and meticulously dusts all the surfaces, then we see him in action. There's no need to tell us how neat and thorough he is. He's very different from the cleaner who shoots round with a damp cloth and has the job done in half an hour, then spends the rest of the shift smoking on the back door-step.

We can also take this a stage further when thinking about our main characters and use the notion of seeing how a character might react in a given situation as a means of testing out a character. The situation we concoct doesn't have to be part of the finished work; we can view it as a kind of exercise to get us thinking about character just like we did with the character questionnaire.

For instance, if one of your characters came home from holiday to find they'd been burgled, what would their reaction be?

Yes, most of us will phone the police, but there are other reactions we could have. A character who is excessively untidy may not even notice that the burglars have been in. On the other hand, one who is über-organised might head straight for the filing cabinet and whip out a pristine inventory of the household contents and begin checking off exactly what's missing. A disorganised character may find they've forgotten to renew the household insurance, a difficult character might argue every tiny point with the insurance company. The person who sits in the middle of the mess weeping uncontrollably is very different from the one who whips out a gun and tours the neighbourhood looking to exact revenge.

Similarly, what would your character do if they won £10,000? This is a much more intriguing question than asking what they would do if they won the lottery jackpot. £10,000 is an interesting sum. For some people it would be entirely life-changing. For others, it would be a drop in the ocean. Will they wipe out debts, give it to charity, buy a car, have a holiday, put it in a savings account, gamble it at the race-track, have a face-lift or a boob job or pay someone to kill off a rival?

It's quite easy to fall into the trap of thinking what we'd do in any given situation and then having our characters do that, but if we put ourselves in their shoes, adopt their mind-set, then we can discover elements of their personality that perhaps hadn't occurred to us.

# Over to you

1. For each of the following character traits and write down a couple of ways in which you could show a character behaving in this way. For instance, if we chose 'tight-fisted', we could have someone open a purse very close to their chest - especially if it's a male character.

- A bully
- A gossip
- Charming, but untrustworthy
- Generous
- Gluttonous
- Greedy
- Intolerant of fools
- Obsessed with the way they look
- Tight-fisted

2. Now think about a specific character you're working on. How would your character react if ....?

- a relative they didn't like came to stay for ages?
- someone broke into their house when they were on holiday?
- someone pushed past them in a queue?
- they accidentally clip off another car's wing-mirror in the car-park?
- they found a £20 note in the street?
- they found out their partner was cheating on them?
- they were arrested for a crime they didn't commit?
- they were given a present they didn't particularly like?
- they were told a secret about someone they didn't particularly like?
- they won £10,000?

# 11

# What makes him tick? Character motivation

Imagine a story where things just happen. We have a protagonist who simply goes through a series of incidents without wanting anything, without needing anything, without anything to cause the slightest ripple across the surface of his day.

He gets up in the morning, has breakfast with his non-squabbling family. Goes off to work in his perfectly reliable and comfortable mid-range car and there are no roadworks or traffic jams on the way. At work, his boss, his co-workers and everyone he meets is perfectly pleasant. He goes online to check his bank balance and finds that he has easily enough money till the end of the month. He buys his wife some flowers, she's pleased with them. He decides to mow the lawn, which was fairly neat any way, but needed a little trim. The mower works just fine and the weather is pleasant enough so he doesn't break out in a sweat. He decides he'll fire up the barbecue and he and his wife share a bottle of wine. He has a good night's sleep and is well-rested for when he gets up in the morning again.

Whilst that sounds like a pretty decent life, and many of us would be contented with such an existence, it's not fiction. No matter how we dress it up, there's no dramatic tension for our main character. Yes, we can write some beautiful prose. You'll be able to hear the buzzing of the lawn-mower, smell the sizzle of the sausages, taste the chilled Chablis as he rolls it round his tongue, but you'll be bored stiff. There's no yearning, nothing missing from that character's life. All the reader is going to say is, 'So what?'

No-one would give a damn. Contentment may be fine in real life, but fiction is not real life. Fiction is where we pile on the agony and make our characters suffer. And we pile on the agony by giving our characters some kind of motivation. At the heart of any character, more important than all the other elements we're looking at in this book, such as physical description, lifestyle, family, general situation, name or backstory, we need motivation. A character must want something. It is the core, the essence, their *raison d'être*. It is the essential ingredient of fiction.

Every major character needs some kind of overall, over-arching goal. If we take two of the staples of fiction, the romance novel and the detective story, it's quite easy to see what the main characters' motivation usually is. In an archetypal romance novel, the girl wants the boy. In detective fiction, the police officer (or occasionally some amateur sleuth) needs to find the perpetrator. There is a simple built-in general motivation in each of these kinds of stories. Similarly, in a western, the sheriff wants to clean up the town. In a heist plot, the ingenious criminals want to make off with a stash of jewels. In an adventure yarn, our hero needs to find the pot of gold or the sleeping princess or the witch who can break the spell.

Robinson Crusoe must want human company. In Herman Melville's *Moby Dick*, Captain Ahab wants revenge on the great white whale that has made off with his leg, leaving him clumping round on one good one and one made (inevitably) from whalebone. Ahab's revenge becomes an obsession as everything that has gone wrong in his life is heaped on Moby Dick's water-spouting head. In F. Scott Fitzgerald's *The Great Gatsby*, Jay Gatsby yearns for Daisy in an obsessional way, angry that she has not kept her promise to him that they would marry after the Great War, but has married Tom Buchanan instead. All of Gatsby's great desire to live a life of wealth and luxury is to prove to Daisy that he is good enough to marry into her refined family. In both these cases, the motivation becomes obsessional to the point of destruction. Even in comedy, we need motivation. Mrs. Bennet in *Pride and Prejudice* has five daughters, all of whom need marrying off. She's motivated by trying to find husbands for them all.

Motivation doesn't have to be obsessional. But it certainly has to be stronger than 'I'd quite like a boyfriend, but it doesn't matter too much' or 'If we don't get him this time, he'll always kill a few more women and he's bound to make a mistake and we might get him at the fifth or sixth attempt'.

Vitally, motivation also needs to be entirely specific. Whilst we can say in general terms that the heroine of a romantic novel wants love, we have to force ourselves to be more precise with our motivation. 'Love' is too vague. She could stick an advert on the Internet and just take up with the first bloke who came along. No, our heroine must want precisely one person. She may waver and dither between two or three choices, as happens to Elizabeth Bennet in *Pride and Prejudice*, but eventually she has to plump for the right one. It's not just any of the three that will do, it has to be Mr. Right, in this case Mr. Darcy. Similarly, our detective isn't going to settle for collaring the Garden Gnome Nabber, when there's a serial killer on the rampage.

## Fear is a great motivational force in fiction: give us some jeopardy

We can quickly establish what your character wants, but the most potent motivational force of all is fear. Fear comes in all shapes and sizes:

- If you don't catch the serial killer, he'll do it again
- If you don't find the bomb, it will go off
- If you don't use clever questioning in court, the criminal will get off scot free
- If you don't find Mr. Right, you'll be the only singleton at the party
- If you don't find work, you'll lose your house
- If we don't get her to the hospital in time, she's going to die

Of course, it's the character's reaction to that fear that makes your character an individual. It is the way in which they go about assuaging their fears that makes us want to read on. If at every twist and turn, you place you character in jeopardy, then you will test them to the full and they will resonate more strongly with the reader.

## Be nasty

You have to be as nasty as you can to your characters. If you make life easy for them, then we can't root for them. Imagine if our serial killer just walked through the door and gave himself up. Where's the dramatic tension there? He's done the detective's work for him. No, we have to put obstacles in his way. If someone does walk in through the door, claiming to be the killer, then it has to be a hoax confession. But it has to be a good hoax. Perhaps the confessor knows details that the police think are not in the public domain. They are pretty convinced until something happens to disabuse them — another killing, the realisation that there is a leak from the police station and gory details are all over a macabre Internet chat-room site. We can throw up other obstacles — a killing that looks initially that it's part of the same sequence, but which isn't. The arrest of a very likely suspect, who turns out to be innocent. Someone lies convincingly to give the real antagonist an alibi.

## Motivation changes

We're going to take a walk further into the dark realms of cliché here in order to illustrate that we also normally need to have a web of motivation.

Your detective may want to catch the killer, but he also wants to spend more time with his children, whom he's been neglecting. Additionally, he needs to find some kind of *modus vivendi* with his ex-wife and his officious superior officer, who is much keener on paperwork than he is. He also has the cloud of a potential internal investigation hanging over him, being led by a policeman whom he knows to be corrupt, so he has to deal with that, whilst at the same time breaking in a new Sergeant, who has all the intellect of a trepanned sheep.

Motivation changes as the story progresses. If your detective finds out who he thinks did it, his motivation then changes from finding the perpetrator to proving him guilty. He does this, but the guilty man walks free from the court on a technicality. So your detective takes the law into his own hands. His motivation is now to kill the villain. He kills the villain. Now his motivation is not to get caught himself. He makes it look like suicide.

Motivation comes in the form of an over-arching goal, and changes as need arises, but also changes for every scene, and importantly within each scene. In addition, every other character in a scene must have some kind of agenda as well.

When our detective calls round to take his children out for the day (this is a staple of all TV detectives!), if the ex-wife hands over the children with the instruction to be back by eight o'clock and everyone gets happily into the car and they have a whizzo day and the kids are returned by quarter to the hour, there is no tension. Everyone has exactly the same motivation, so there is no conflict to increase the drama. It's lawn-mowing-barbecue-husband all over again.

To ramp up the tension, we can imagine that we might have the following sets of motivation:

- The ex-wife is annoyed because the detective's late. But it's not just that he's late, she also knows that her new beau she's trying to keep quiet about could now arrive at any moment. The beau is organised for 10.30 and one of the things she finds attractive about him is that he's more punctual than her ex ever was. She doesn't want ex-husband/detective to know about the new man – could be because he'll reduce child-care or even run a police check on the new man.

- The older child doesn't want to spend the day with our detective, but wants to be with her friends. She's also decided that she's a vegetarian because her best friend is.
- The younger child wants to be with him, and likes the idea of going to a burger restaurant as she has been collecting the plastic toys they've been giving away.
- The estranged wife wants both children to go with him, but doesn't want him to go to the burger bar as she'd like him to take them somewhere she feels gives them a more balanced diet.
- The younger child also fancies a cartoon at the cinema, but the older child thinks this is too babyish, so that even when she's been persuaded/cajoled/coerced into going, she wants to go and see the live action film with the latest boy band in it.
- Then the ex-wife's new boyfriend arrives. He's motivated by lust. But he doesn't realise until this point that ex-husband is a copper and he could have his unsavoury past unmasked to his new lady-friend.

Yes, it's hackneyed. Yes, you've seen it often before, but the point is that everyone has a motivation in the scene. It also creates conflict, and without conflict we have no drama, we just have barbecuing and lawn-mowing and sips of Chablis.

We'll deal more fully with writing dialogue later on, but bear in mind that writing exchanges between characters also tends to force us to write in scenes, which is good for any work of fiction. We move out of the characters' heads and ensure that we have something cinematic going on. It also helps us to develop the conflicts between characters and, as Kurt Vonnegut says in one of *The Paris Review Interviews*, 'it is the writer's job to stage confrontations, so the characters will say surprising and revealing things, and educate and entertain us all. If a writer can't or won't do that, he should withdraw from the trade.'

Any scene you write should advance the plot, of course, and make us want to read on to find out what happens next. But it must also show us conflict between characters. As writers, we know we have to expose ourselves and dig deep into our own well of memories and emotions to give the reader the full-blown experience that our characters are undergoing. This will help give our characters motivation for everything they do.

## Over to you

Ask yourself the following questions about each of your characters:

- What do they want?
- How are they going to get it?
- How ruthless are they going to be?
- Who (or what) is going to stop them from getting it?
- Why should the reader care?

# 12

# Making your characters talk

Have you ever had the misfortune to read the kind of book where we have page after page of a character's dull thoughts interspersed with meandering, unfocused description? You're desperate for one of the characters to say something. Anything. Just one word. You flick ahead, looking for any sign of an inverted comma, but no, no luck. Do you plough on, trapped because you're the sort of person who just has to finish a book once they've started it? Or do you add the book to the pile of emergency fuel should there be a power-cut.

When you come across huge dry stretches of barren dialogue-free prose, you realise how vital dialogue is to a book. Without dialogue, we can't expect any of our characters to seem like real people. Catching their tone of voice, the rhythms of what they say and their vocabulary is what pulls in the reader and makes them believe that these characters are flesh and blood.

There are other, technical advantages to writing dialogue too. When the people in your book speak, this is a way of introducing sound via the reader's head, meaning you've automatically added another of the five senses to your writing.

In addition, speech obviously occurs when our various characters interact, so this helps us write in scenes (and thus show rather than tell). As John Singleton stresses in *The Creative Writing Workbook*, 'Good dialogue does give **immediacy** to fiction. It shows things as they happen.'

And, silly though it may seem, the fact that speech tends to come in little bursts, means that we get in more paragraph indents and short lines, which creates more white space on the page and actually makes a book physically easier to read.

When we're writing dialogue, we need to bear in mind that it must do one of three things:

- give us information
- move the story along
- tell us about character

Of course, if you can manage to do all three of these together, then that's tremendous. The worst kind of dialogue gives us none of these. I was once handed a script in which one of the characters checked into a country hotel and then spent five minutes discussing with the barman what would be best to eat for his evening meal. It went something along these lines:

*Man: What's on the menu tonight?*
*Barman: We have sausages, lasagne, scampi, liver and bacon.*
*Man: What kind of sausages are they?*
*Barman: They're Lincolnshire sausages, as you're asking.*
*Man: And is the lasagne beef or lamb?*
*Barman: Beef.*
*Man: Mmm. Good, I like beef.*

... and so on until all the possibilities had been exhausted and I had taken to drinking hard liquor.

When I (politely) asked the author why they'd taken a page or more on this dialogue, they replied, 'Well, he's got to eat something hasn't he?' Of course he does, but the author didn't have a scene where the main man defecated, and after all that food...

Not only does this dialogue exchange not move the story anywhere, but it has the added distinction of not telling us anything about the characters or the situation, save for the fascinating facts that the pub has a fairly limited menu and our main man likes beef. Neither of these were hidden plot-points either, as no-one was poisoned and our main man didn't develop BSE in

Chapter 16 due to his preference for beef.

If the scene had been written differently, we might have had a character telling us that he can't eat any of that lot, because he's vegetarian, or has a wheat allergy, or we could have it made amusing by an inability to choose. The reality is that it's just padding. It's the writer warming up to the task of getting characters on the page and finding out what they sound like. There's nothing wrong with writing a scene like this to help you get a fix on the people in your story, but once you've written in, it needs to be either cut or re-written in such a way as it gives us something useful, according to our three principles above – information, moving the story along, character.

This is an extreme example, but it's still always worth looking through your dialogue to make sure that what is on the page is there for a purpose. To help, you can use the thought processes actors go through at this stage. For every line an actor speaks, there has to be a single motivation for it. Why is a character saying this? What do they hope to gain as a result? If the line carries no weight, then it's probably as well to cut it.

## An ear for dialogue

For some writers, dialogue flows easily. Everything they write sounds like somebody speaking. Their dialogue rolls easily off the tongue, it has rhythm. It sounds natural. We praise them for 'having an ear for dialogue'.

In fact what they have done is to perform a neat trick. What these people realise is that first and foremost, dialogue has to maintain the pretence that it is people speaking, rather than be the real thing.

What they have written is not natural at all. Natural speech is largely gibberish if written on the page. If you have ever read a transcription of people speaking, it's almost impossible to follow. It certainly isn't something you would want to read for pure enjoyment. Check the verbatim report of any court case or recordings of telephone calls or even the famous Nixon tapes, and you'll see that we human beings um and err. We say the same thing several times over. We don't follow formal sentence structure. We break off mid-thought, go off at tangents, mishear or misuse words. When our real speech is written down, we all sound like babbling, incoherent morons.

If you want to check this out for yourself, record a telephone conversation. You'll find you get exchanges like this:

*It's me ... you all right, cause ... she came over ... but ... the thing's not there, you know...*

*No... yeah ... no, fine ... it's, you know, sorted ... he was like ...*

*I might not...*

*No. Me too. I'm not sure ... I think ... well ... I'm not sure.*

Frankly, it's annoying. In fact, it's more than annoying; it's entirely pointless, because the reader doesn't have the first clue about what's happening.

However, if you go too far the other way and write dialogue that is perfectly grammatical and too precise and your characters will all sound far too stilted, far too formal. At best, they'll sound like a bad US TV film version of an Oxford don. Writing dialogue is a tricky business. It's not just a question of sticking some inverted commas round a chunk of text and passing it off as the spoken word. The flat-pack approach to dialogue would have our character say:

*She: Before assembling the shelving, ensure that you have all the correct components. You will also need a flat-head screw-driver, a cross-head screwdriver, a size 9 spanner and a small hammer. Lay components A, B and C on the floor, as in diagram 1, ensuring that you have parts D, E and F to hand. Insert D into A, E into B and F into C, as per diagram 2.*

*He: Could you possibly repeat that for my benefit as my attention was elsewhere?*

What writers faced with having to write a flat-pack scene would have to do is something like this:

*She: Have you got all the parts?*
  *He: Yes, of course.*
  *She: Have you checked?*
  *He: Pass me the screw-driver. No, not that one the other one ...*
  *She: That's not what it shows you in the diagram.*
  *He: We don't need little pictures. It's a set of shelves. How hard can it be?*

... and so forth. What we've done here is to take what feels like natural speech, but left out all the awkwardness of it, such as the half-finished sentences, hesitations and repetitions, whilst attempting to move our story (such as it is) forward.

You can test out whether it feels all right by reading it out loud. Can you actually speak it without stumbling over the words? If you can't, then it needs re-writing. Of course, you may decide the scene isn't relevant at all, and have to cut it altogether, which is probably what I'd be tempted to do with the flat-pack scene above.

## What does your character sound like?

In her fabulous book *Watching the English*, Kate Fox explains how you can check on someone's social class. You just have to say something a little bit too quietly for a person to hear you properly:

*A lower-middle or middle-middle class person will say 'Pardon?'; an upper-middle will say 'Sorry?' (or perhaps 'Sorry –what?' or 'What – sorry?'); but an upper-class and a working-class person will both just say 'What?'. The working-class person may drop the 't' — 'Wha'?' —*

*but this will be the only difference.*

Fox lists 'pardon' as one of the seven deadly sins that mean that the upper-classes can spot a pleb straight away. The other six words are toilet (for lavatory), serviette (for napkin), dinner (for lunch), settee (for sofa), lounge (for sitting-room or drawing room) and sweet (for pudding). Of course, this is about the English and your characters may well hail from elsewhere, but the point is made that even with such tiny indicators, we can guide the reader as to where our characters stand on the social scale.

## Dealing with dialect

Our flat-pack shelf-builders are speaking a pretty standard version of English. What do you do if your characters speak differently to that? British English is rich in different accents and dialects, before we even start thinking about English spoken in the rest of the world.

The Scottish novelist Irvine Welsh is unafraid to have his characters talk in the broadest of dialects. In his novel *Filth*, the dialogue is seamed directly into the narrative without the use of traditional punctuation methods. Here, the speaker is a sociopath policeman, who is introducing Maisie, a brothel's madam and ex-prostitute, to his younger colleague, Ray:

*-Tell ye what Ray, Maisie here, she'd teach ye things that yir ma couldnae. Forgotten mair thin you're ever ever likely tae learn. Ah keep tryin tae entice her back oot ay retirement, but she's havin nane ay it.*

Throughout the book, the dialogue — and indeed the narrative voice — is all written in heavy dialect, laced with the strongest of swear-words, which are also integral to the characters.

There's a strong tradition of trying to render dialect phonetically. Irvine Welsh is not the only Scottish author to do this —

James Kelman and even Walter Scott do something similar. Authors in the literary canon, such as D. H. Lawrence and Emily Brontë have also written wodges of speech in difficult-to-follow dialect. In *Lady Chatterley's Lover*, the gamekeeper Mellors slips from using standard English — he may be a gamekeeper, but he also held a commission in the British army — into a broad Midlands dialect in order to stress the social difference between himself and Constance Chatterley. He liked a bit of inverted snobbery did D. H.

Writing in broad dialect is a risky business. The language and spelling can be extremely hard to follow. Writers who use it are striving for deliberate effect. Strip away Welsh's deliberate evocation of place and people through his use of language and speech patterns and you remove a vital layer from the stories. For me, this is what makes them great; others will be less convinced.

There are several additional problems with writing in dialect. If it isn't your natural speech, you can get it very badly wrong and it will chime falsely with people for whom that is their natural speech pattern, or who have been brought up in a particular region and know it well.

It's also extremely difficult for people who don't know a local accent to understand what you've written. If you write 'Ars gan yam temorrer', it might be recognised by half of the people living in Cumbria as meaning 'I'm going home tomorrow.' Most of us might understand the 'temorrer', but are probably clueless as to what the rest of the sentence means. On the other hand, if you write ' "I'm going home tomorrow," he said in his Cumbrian accent,' readers can then apply their own version of Cumbrian to what you've written. And, if their version of Cumbrian is Yorkshire or Lancashire or Geordie or even BBC multi-purpose Northern, then it doesn't really matter. Besides, there's a wide variety of accents in Cumbria. Someone from Barrow-in-Furness sounds nothing like someone from Carlisle.

## Swearing

The Irvine Welsh snippet above was also partly chosen because it is a rare passage without heavy-duty swearing. Sometimes, when I'm running workshops, the subject of swearing comes up. Some people are still deeply offended by what they see as 'bad language'. If you're one of those people, then you probably won't feel comfortable if you have foul-mouthed characters wreaking havoc in your fiction. Fine. Just don't write the kinds of characters who are likely to swear a great deal. Regency romances don't go in for bad language, despite the fact that the era had some of the greatest slang words ever coined, especially for male and female genitalia. On the other hand, if your character is a thuggish armed robber, he's hardly likely to say such things as, 'Golly, crikey, lummy, I've been shot in the testicles. Lawks how that hurts.'

## A caveat — dialogue in fiction is not film dialogue

When we watch films or TV dramas, the dialogue is, by several furlongs, in second place to the visuals. With a film, it's what we see that does the vast majority of the work. Scriptwriters tend to work out all their basic scenes before adding in a single line of speech. Read a movie script and it's a series of instructions for the director to follow. The dialogue is pared back as far as it possibly can be, allowing the camera to be the real pen. If a character can be shown nodding their head in agreement, then even the word 'yes' will be left out.

We can follow the pantomiming of early films easily. The entire heist scene in the French film *Rififi* is almost entirely silent, even to the extent of having no musical score. Likewise in the opening of Hitchcock's *Rear Window*, the camera roves voyeuristically across the windows and balconies of a roasting hot New York morning and establishes a huge amount of information, with a minimum of dialogue, about the residents of the apartments opposite Jimmy Stewart's living-room window. The camera also lingers across Stewart's collection of photographs, personal possessions and the plaster cast on his leg before we get to hear him speak.

In the caper movie, *The Italian Job*, we see Charlie Croker (Michael Caine) and one of his criminal gang poised with a detonating device in his hand. Croker is training up his boys for a bullion robbery in Italy. As Croker counts down, the camera zooms in number by number on the van until it explodes magnificently. Then Croker says, 'You're only supposed to blow the bloody doors off!' The camera has done so much of the work; that the simple one-liner becomes hugely memorable.

## Another caveat — dialogue in fiction is not stage dialogue

At school, we often study older novels, where the dialogue is wordier than in their modern counterparts, or plays, where speech is embedded in what the actors do as we see them move around the stage.

The dialogue of novels and stories is not quite the same beast as stage dialogue.

Stage dialogue tends to carry more information than film dialogue. Unless you had the world's biggest stage budget, if you want to re-enact the sinking of the Titanic on-stage, you'd have characters pointing out above the audience, shouting:

*'That's an iceberg!'*
*'She's breaking up!'*
*'Oh my God, we're sinking!'*
*'Women and children first! Lieutenant Smithers, what are you doing in that frock?'*

Whereas in a film, you don't need any of this, as you can pay your special effects team to recreate it all for you.

Stage dialogue, however, like film dialogue is contextualised by the actors, the set, costumes and so forth. Take this dialogue exchange from the opening of David Mamet's *Speed-the-Plow*, for example. The two main characters here are described simply as 'Bobby Gould, Charlie Fox, two men around forty' and the setting is just 'Gould's office, morning'. What follows includes the few stage directions as they appear in my Methuen copy, because without them, I suspect we're entirely at sea:

*Gould's office. Morning. Boxes and painting materials all around. Gould is sitting, reading, Fox enters.*
  *Gould: When the gods make us mad, they answer our prayers.*
  *Fox: Bob...*
  *Gould: I'm in the midst of the wilderness.*
  *Fox: Bob ...*
  *Gould: If it's not quite "Art" and it's not quite "Entertainment", it's here on my desk. I have inherited a monster.*
  *Fox: ... Bob ...*
  *Gould (leafing through the book he is reading, reads): "A certain frankness came to it ..." (He leafs.) "The man, downcast, then met the priest, under the bridge which stood for so much, where so much had transpired since the radiation."*
  *Fox: ... yeah, Bob, that's great ...*
  *Gould: Listen to this: "and with it brought grace. But still the questions persisted ... that of the Radiation. That of the growth of animalism, the decay of the soil. And it said 'Beyond terror. Beyond grace' ... and caused a throbbing ... machines in the void ..." (He offers the book to Fox.) Here: take a page.*
  *Fox: I have to talk to you.*

I suspect that most of you felt rather lost reading though that. There are minimal stage directions (unlike, for instance, plays from the 1920s). There's very little here to give us an idea of context. Nor do we have any detailed description of what these men look like. Are they wearing suits or jeans? Are they lean and healthy or flabby and out-of-condition?

Relying on our familiarity with stage dialogue from studying plays at school isn't always that helpful. Speech in fiction tends to be neither the wordy dialogue of Shakespeare, nor the entirely leaner prose of modern dramatists that relies on the actor to give meaning to what is said. As a fiction writer, if you want to write the scene such as the one we have between Fox and Gould, then you need to help your reader along a little. We need more context. We need to be given a portrait of the scene and we also need to have some indication of how the two men talk. When Bob complains of work that falls between being art and entertainment sitting on his desk, we would need to see the pile of scripts, see him wave his arm around. When he reads, is he being sarcastic, puzzled or physically revolted by what is in the script?

If we were to recreate this scene as a piece of fiction, the temptation is to write a bit of set-piece description. For example, we'll see the pots of paint in Bob's office, the way the sun comes through the blind, which walls have been painted and so on and then we'll see what Bob and Charlie look like, then we'll have some ping-ponging dialogue.

We need to avoid the trap of thinking that the shape of a scene looks like this:

- Describe setting
- Describe Person 1
- Describe Person 2
- Dialogue

Whereas what we need to do is to integrate them, so that the character and all the elements that go to help us visualise that character are interwoven.

## On the other hand — what we can learn from scriptwriters

What we can learn from scriptwriters is that our dialogue needs to remain to the point. A scriptwriter will make every single word of dialogue count. As writers, we need to focus on what our characters are saying.

Often, fiction writers pad their dialogue. Too often we are given stodgy, lengthy speeches which rarely ring true. It's quite unbelievable when one character talks for a page or more, unless they're actually telling a story or giving a lecture. And that's when we can fall into another trap:

## The danger of the infodump

We have some vital information that the reader needs to know and we realise that dialogue can be used to get across information. In an attempt to create a dramatic scene, instead of writing pure narrative summary, we just give it to a character and wrap some speech marks around it. Spew out a load of information and we call this the 'infodump':

*'I don't think you've met my cousin Barry. He used to be in the army, but was wounded in the Gulf. Despite only having an invalidity pension and being a widower — remember that his wife ran off with the man from the Co-op — he's managed to bring up his two daughters. He lives over in Suffolk in a semi-detached house, where he spends his time water-colour painting and studying Feng Shui.'*

Pass the ammunition. You can occasionally get away with a character doling out raw information, but it tends to be best to do so in a situation where this would occur naturally. There are countless war films where the flight crew is briefed about what's going to happen, with the Group Captain tapping his stick on a pull-down map of the Ruhrland. Cowboy films are rarely complete without a scene where the cavalry officer takes a stick and draws a plan of attack in the sand.

You can use such situations as teachers in school classrooms, academics in lecture theatres, priests in pulpits, managers in meetings, delegates at conferences, guides on tour buses, politicians on soap-boxes, announcers on television or mentors guiding new recruits round the facilities to drop in pure information. The rule-of-thumb is that an infodump should be kept short and pertinent. Most importantly, let's have something of the character come through what is actually said. If you do this, you can also have a bit of fun with them by giving them a few unusual characteristics.

Give the speaker some kind of attitude. For instance, O'Brien, Winston Smith's torturer, gives us raw information as he prepares the cage full of rats in Room 101 (*1984*, George Orwell):

*'The rat,' said O'Brien, still addressing his invisible audience, 'although a rodent, is carnivorous. You are aware of that. You will have heard of the things that happen in the poorer quarters of this town. In some streets a woman dare not leave her baby alone in the house, even for five minutes. The rats are certain to attack it. Within quite a small time they will strip it to the bones. They also attack sick or dying people. They show astonishing intelligence in knowing when a human being is helpless.'*

Of course, this is far less about the habits of rats than it is an extreme threat to Winston Smith. The calculation and coldness of the speech are in direct contrast to the idea that Smith will be squirming in absolute terror, whilst his torturer, ramps up the fear.

## Yet another caveat — the danger of Q & A

In an attempt to get over a solid block of information, we can then divide it up, parcelling out the information between characters. If we're not careful, this can lead to clumsy question-

and-answer:

*Friend: How's your new colleague?*
*Heroine: He seems very nice.*
*Friend: When did he start?*
*Heroine: Last Monday.*
*Friend: Where did he work before?*
*Heroine: He was in the finance department of Smith and Sons.*
*Friend: Where are they?*
*Heroine: They're based in Colchester.*

Here, the friend's only rôle is to serve up questions for our heroine to answer. Yes, it's an attempt to make a scene come to life, but it's halting and it seems unnatural and clumsy. We can also fall into the trap of having our have characters telling people what they already know and have dialogue that simply ping-pongs its way down the page.

There are occasions when you can use the question-and-answer technique, but these are best left to situations where people would genuinely be using questions and answers, such as in a job interview. Even then, if all you do is rely on straight-forward Q & A, it will become boring for the reader.

We can try to get round this difficulty by embedding information in something that feels like a genuine conversation. Should you wish to try to breathe life into the raw facts about this new chap, where he worked before and so forth, you could try something along these lines:

*Friend: He looks all right, your new colleague.*
**We get in the info that there's a new colleague. 'All right' might mean dishy/pleasant/a good worker — readers can decide. Friend may even fancy him.**
*Heroine: I'm having chips. I don't care.*
**She changes the subject. Maybe she fancies him, but doesn't**

*want to let on. She's possibly a bit overweight, or should at least be trying to eat better.*

Friend: Life-time on the hips ...

**Yes, it looks even more likely she's overweight, and her friend also likes to rub it in.**

Heroine: Give it a rest.

**Changing subject didn't work — the friend is possibly slimmer and better-looking.**

Friend: I bet you would, though, if he asked you.

**Readers can interpret this as sex/going out/marriage, let them do part of the work.**

Heroine: You haven't heard him speak. He sounds like an East End gangster. Are we ready to order?

**Bit of snobbery here, plus we get some geographical information. Another change of subject, plus we're embedding it in the reality of the scene — getting a meal.**

It's not the world's best dialogue exchange, but at least we're trying to do something a bit more with this scene. Even better would be to think of a more interesting situation in the first place.

If handled cleverly, then sharp exchanges of question-and-answer can work extremely well. In the following extract from Joseph Heller's *Catch-22*, Yossarian, nerves shattered by too many bombing missions, visits Doc Daneeka in an attempt to have himself declared unfit for flying:

'Can't you ground someone who's crazy?' [said Yossarian]

'Oh, sure, I have to. There's a rule saying I have to ground anyone who's crazy.'

'Then why don't you ground me? I'm crazy. Ask Clevinger.'

'Clevinger? Where is Clevinger? You find Clevinger and I'll ask him.'

'Then ask any of the others. They'll tell you how crazy I am.'

*'They're crazy.'*

*'Then why don't you ground them?'*

*'Why don't they ask me to ground them?'*

*'Because they're crazy, that's why.'*

*'Of course they're crazy,'* Doc Daneeka replied. *'I just told you they're crazy, didn't I? And you can't let crazy people decide whether you're crazy or not, can you?'*

Yossarian looked at him soberly and tried another approach. *'Is Orr crazy?'*

*'He sure is,'* Doc Daneeka said.

*'Can you ground him?'*

*'I sure can. But first he has to ask me to. That's part of the rule.'*

*'Then why doesn't he ask you to?'*

*'Because he's crazy,'* Doc Daneeka said. *'He has to be crazy to keep flying combat missions after all the close calls he's had. Sure, I can ground Orr. But first he has to ask me to.'*

*'That's all he has to do to be grounded?'*

*'That's all. Let him ask me.'*

*'And then you can ground him?'* Yossarian asked.

*'No. Then I can't ground him.'*

*'You mean there's a catch?'*

*'Sure there's a catch,'* Doc Daneeka replied. *'Catch-22. Anyone who wants to get out of combat duty isn't really crazy.'*

There's a Kafkaesque circularity to all this, which means that we can feel Yossarian's frustration searing off the page. It's also interesting to note how little narrative, or even speech-markers, surrounds this exchange. Heller allows the dialogue to do all the work.

## He said/she said

One of the newest writer's biggest fears is how to show who is speaking. When they write a scene that involves a lot of dialogue, they look over what they've written and the word 'said' seems to appear far too often. Surely the reader must be fed up with the sight of it?

Surprisingly, readers don't tend to notice the word 'said' at all. It's almost as though it were a punctuation mark, just a little means of guiding the reader. However, the newer writer, fearing this may not be the case, starts looking for alternative words. Eventually nobody 'says' anything, because they're too busy suggesting, shouting, screaming, whispering, moaning, conjecturing, confiding, guessing, deliberating or, in the wonderful world of the late Georgette Heyer, ejaculating.

Unless you're writing deliberately purple prose for people who will only read one book a year then apart from 'said', you might also be allowed 'replied', 'asked', 'shouted', 'whispered', but be really strict on yourself about the other variations.

If you think you've got too many speech tags (he said/she said), you can always use the age-old trick of having one for the characters do something and attach what they say to the action:

*Julie made her way over to the corner table. 'Sorry, I'm late.'*

*'Not your new boss keeping you late, is it?' Helen moved her coat and bag out of the way as Julie sat down.*

This way, we know Julie says 'Sorry I'm late' and Helen mentions the boss keeping Julie back.

Another neat trick to get over the he said/she said business is for characters to use other characters' names a little more than they might in real life.

*Julie made her way over to the corner table. 'Sorry, I'm late, Helen.'*

*'Not your new boss keeping you late, is it?' Helen moved her coat and bag out of the way as Julie sat down.*

*They inspected the menu for a minute.*

*'So what are you having, Helen?'*

It has to be Julie who makes that last speech, as we only have two people in the scene.

## Over to you

Without using any speech tags, write a pure dialogue using one of the following scenarios or if you prefer, invent one of your own:

- The doctor attending a boy who has recently died asks his bereaved mother if she is prepared to allow her son's organs to be used for transplant.
- Two children are playing in a graveyard. One wants to try to open a half-broken tomb, the other doesn't.
- A person who has happily been living alone in some remote part of the country (a mountain goatherd, a lighthouse keeper, the warden of a tiny island) suddenly has to cope with a new arrival.
- A customer brings back an item of clothing that has clearly been worn, demanding a refund.

When you've done this, read it out loud. If you can get a friend to help, even better. Check the following:

- Does it sound like real speech? (In the accepted sense for drama/fiction purposes.)
- Does every line give us information, move the story on or tell us about character?
- Have you got any lines that do all three? (Bonus points for that.)
- When is it carrying pure information? Is this reasonably well hidden?
- What could you cut/improve on a second draft?

# 13

## What does your character think?
## (And how does she think it?)

Fiction writers have one method of character representation that is not available to the playwright or the screenwriter; they can actually go inside the head of their characters and tell the reader exactly what's going on.

Sure, in a play or film, an actor can display an emotion. They can kick a car when it doesn't start or cradle a crying baby and we know that they're angry or have a soft side. But we can't actually hear their thoughts. There are occasionally tricksy exceptions, such as in the film *Annie Hall*, where the Diane Keaton and Woody Allen characters are talking and what they're really thinking appears in a series of subtitles. There is also the old standby of the soliloquy. When Hamlet debates suicide, we are privy to his innermost thoughts, but again this is an obvious device and never feels entirely realistic. The same is true, to an extent of the cinematic equivalent of the soliloquy, the voice-over, which some people find extremely annoying — perhaps because it breaks the pretence of watching real life.

Only in prose fiction, do we have the opportunity to enter a character's mind without feeling as though we're doing so through the medium of some artistic contrivance. This has both advantages as well as pitfalls. Let's deal with the latter first.

One of the greatest disadvantages is that the luxury of being able to go inside a character's head means that it's very tempting to spend a lot of time in there. Frankly, it's pretty easy to take us on a tour of the interior of your protagonist's cranium. We can take a page, or two, or whole chapter, to waffle on about how upset poor Hermione is with her mother's behaviour and how she's never shown her the love she showed the other children and how if she could maybe see the bank manager, she might just be able to explain why she's so badly in debt, which she wouldn't be if it hadn't have been for the vets' bills, but a labradoodle is not just a pet, it's a life companion... and whilst the reader wades through all this dull solipsism, all Hermione has done is pour herself a cup of (decaffeinated) tea. Then off we go again, with the story of her bullying at school, her allergies (lavender bags, inexpensive perfume and pot pourri, but only when there's an "r" in the month), how she deals with his dysmenorrhea, her two ex-husbands, the insolent attitude of the people at the bus-stop last Thursday, when it was raining so hard. By which time, she's nibbled the end of a Bath Oliver biscuit. Then, off we go for another five pages.

Yes, the trouble is that when we're traveling through Hermione's tangled neural pathways, nothing else is happening. There's no action, nothing for us to get excited about.

I'm sure that being badly mothered, dealing with labradoodles or ex-husbands and even eating expensive biscuits could all be made dramatic, but not when we have them mediated through the thoughts of a character. We want to see that maternal cruelty, feel the barbs of her wit, sneeze our way through her allergies and watch her begging for money at the bank.

It's also on occasions like this that we often have the forced intrusion of backstory:

## Backstory – when your character remembers the past

The difficulty is that we need our characters to feel rounded and complete. When we meet them, we want to know that they have had previous lives, that the things that they have experienced have gone some way to making them the people they are today.

Getting in some backstory can be tricky. We can borrow from the films and put in a flashback.

*We know our hero is troubled by something. The camera pans through the greenery surrounding a small pond, over the soundtrack, echoing eerily comes the lone voice of a child singing. 'Hush my baby, don't say a word, Papa's going to buy you a mocking-bird'. We see two young-sters run long a wooden pier and dive-bomb the surface of the pond.*

Yes, it's the perennial favourite, the watery-death-of-a-sibling flashback, complete with nursery rhyme soundtrack. Our hero will always be troubled because of the death of that sibling/friend. It's why he's allowed to do so much moping.

Sandra Newman and Howard Mittelmark warn that 'characters can be provided with some history. But the relationship between that history and their behaviours should be more complex than Pavlovian dog psychology.' If you find that your central character does the human equivalent of salivating every time a bell rings, you need to start thinking at a slightly deeper level. In the case above, we might find our hero staring wistfully into the middle distance every time he comes across an expanse of water. Yuck.

It's easy to fall into the trap of facile backstory, such as using some bit of psychobabble as a means of explaining a character's actions and even easier to do it if you stay in the character's head to get it all out.

The trouble is that too often, we end up with clumsy prose that tells us about the characters' past lives using that most awkward of verb tenses, the pluperfect (he had been/she had eaten/they had driven).

*She realised when she met him that they had come across each other before. He had been a student back then and she had had a summer job waiting tables. They had once been going to go to a movie together, but for some reason this had been cancelled and they had had to do something else instead.*

It's another reason to try to stay out of the character's head as much as possible. Besides, there are other techniques you can use to give your characters a weighty history. You can play with chronology, for instance, as Michael Ondaatje does in *The English Patient*, and move backwards and forward across time, enabling the reader to learn more about our characters on the way.

Backstory also takes us out of the moment. It slows down the pace of the story. Of course, this can occasionally be to our advantage, but your job as a writer is to make us care about the people in your story, so we turn the page. Besides, during internalizations such as this, the writer inevitably falls back on telling us what's going on, rather than showing us. Actions speak louder than words and words speak louder than thoughts. Again, we come back to the mantras of 'show don't tell', 'write in scenes' and 'think cinema film'.

There are also advantages to hearing a character's thoughts and we can make good use of them. The first is obvious, but bears stating baldly: we know for sure what a character is thinking. This gives us the possibility of introducing some dramatic irony. If what the character says or does is in direct contrast to what they're thinking, then we can understand the dissonance more fully and the reader is offered something more complex than it would be without being privy to those thoughts.

The character's thoughts can also help misdirect the reader. Our hero thinks his wife is seeing another man, but we know she's actually taking piano lessons in secret.

## How do we report a character's thoughts?

If we do decide to write what a character is thinking, what's our best way to do it?

We have three essential methods at our disposal. The first method is the narrative summary. The writer simply tells he reader what the character is thinking:

*Deirdre looked at Arthur and thought he was very handsome.*

This method stays very much on the surface. It feels as though we might even have an omniscient narrator at work. Importantly, it doesn't feel close up; we're not inside the character's head. It's back to the old business of telling rather than showing.

The second is via indirect thought:

*Deirdre looked at Arthur. How come she'd never noticed how handsome he was before now?*

This takes us closer into the character, but we're still not allowing the reader completely inside Deirdre's mind. The third method allows us direct access into the characters' head, almost as though they were speaking the words out loud. This is sometimes termed 'overheard thoughts'.

*Deirdre looked at Arthur. My God he's handsome.*

Although there are advantages to all three, if you want your reader to be living Deirdre's journey entirely vicariously, then this is the method to choose. It takes us in as close as we can possibly get.

You may have been taught at school the technique of putting character's thoughts inside inverted commas, almost as though they are speaking aloud what they're thinking

*'Oh my God, he's so handsome,' she thought.*

This has dropped out of fashion, perhaps because it is slightly cumbersome and, as we learn to read in more sophisticated ways, we are able to work out for ourselves when we have slipped inside a character's head.

## Thinking like an actor (again)

Whilst we're doing all this thinking, it's also worth remembering that the more we can think like our characters do, the more we can understand them and make them come alive on the page.

There are certain actors who immerse themselves so fully in the parts they play that for the duration of filming they don't 'come out of character' at all. Amongst those who use this technique is Daniel Day Lewis. On the set of *Lincoln*, he stayed in character for three months and even the film's director Steven Spielberg had to address him as 'Mr. President'. He also, it appears, did something similar in *My Left Foot*, the story of Christy Brown who had cerebral palsy, but went on to be a celebrated artist and writer despite the fact he only had physical control over his famous left foot. Apparently, Day Lewis stayed so much in character that he had to be pushed round the set and fed by the crew.

Now, this may seem extreme, but at the time of writing, he is the only person to have won Best Actor three times, so it's obviously a technique that works — at least for him.

I don't suggest that if your main character is an axe-wielding maniac that you follow suit by getting completely into character. Hacking away at your friends and neighbours is not the ideal way to win respect and might even get you into trouble with the authorities. At the very least, people will stop talking to you. However, by immersing yourself in his (or her) axe-wielding world, you are forcing yourself to feel, think and act as that character would. Why would someone who's been motoring through life quietly, suddenly raid his own tool shed and start on the people around him?

We saw earlier how important motivation is for creating a character. It's important for actors too. They need to understand what drives the people whose skins they're trying to inhabit, so we can learn a great deal from how actors approach a script. When an actor is expected to show great emotion, they draw on their past experiences of certain events. Whilst you may not have ever encountered a road accident, if your character has to deal with a motorway shunt, you can delve back into your own memory and force to the surface emotions that the character will feel — fear, panic, horror, revulsion. Then, you can be truly thinking like your characters.

However, if you find that this doesn't work for you, you can always fall back on Evelyn Waugh. When asked why he never described what his characters were thinking, Evelyn Waugh replied that he did not know what they were thinking; he only knew what they said and did (P D James, *Talking about Detective Fiction*).

## Over to you

1. Write a passage in which we go inside a character's thoughts when what they're doing is in complete contrast to their real nature. For example, normally, they're a careful driver, but they are forced to take someone they dislike as a passenger and so decide to drive like a lunatic. Write the interior monologue for that character.

2. Hot-seating. Here's a technique that's often used in drama to help an actor start inhabiting the character they're trying to play. Normally, the actor will sit in a chair facing other actors who are in a semi-circle, almost like an extremely large interview panel. The semi-circle throws out questions to the actor, who has to answer them as though they are the character they're playing. You might not be able to find a gang of people to throw questions at you. You might also alienate your nearest and dearest if you do, but we can do it as a paper exercise.

3. Take one of your characters and try to imagine that you are that character made flesh. Indeed, you might like to drop back to the character questionnaire to make yourself a list of questions and add some of your own invention to this

list. Ask yourself the following questions:

- Who do you most admire? Why?
- If you could change one thing about your life, what would that be?
- When were you happiest?
- Do you think people should do more to help themselves rather than relying on the state?
- Who was your best teacher at school?
- What do you think about fox-hunting?
- What piece of advice would you give to your children?
- What's the nicest thing anyone has ever said to you?
- What do you do when you've got a heavy cold?
- What annoys you most?
- What would be your ideal Sunday afternoon?
- Where would you like to go for your next holiday?
- How do you get on with modern technology?

# 14

# Who's telling this story? Point-of-view and voice

At the risk of insulting your intelligence and knowledge, let's just take a look at what we mean by point-of-view. Point-of-view refers to the person through whose eyes we see a story unfold. The term 'point-of-view' is interchangeable with 'viewpoint' to all intents and purposes in this context.

Most stories are told either in the third person singular (he or she) or the first person singular (I). You can, of course, mix up the different narrative voices, especially if you move focus from one central character to another. This often happens with third person narratives, where we will have several different focus characters.

### Omniscient and Objective Narrators

There's a form of third person story-telling that we call the omniscient narrator. You will see it often in Victorian literature, where the author — or a disguised version of the author — plays God by knowing absolutely everything that is going on. We dip in and out of different characters' thoughts, as well as seeing them in action. It seems a little old-fashioned now, and the danger of using it is that we don't stay close enough to the characters. It's still occasionally used in short stories, where we get the set-up, before we get inside the mind of a single character. Often the author will give the narrator a certain 'voice':

*They were staying at the Madeira Lodge, which despite sounding like a sub-tropical paradise was in the kind of area where you needed to walk around in threes. Frank looked at his wife and wondered how on earth she'd managed to book them into this grubby cockroach pit, especially given the reviews of the place on the Internet. He was tired. She was tried. Hell, I'm even tired trying to remember it all.*

It perhaps feels a little too knowing for a realistic novel, although you'll often find it in meta-fiction, where the reader is always being made aware of the fact that they're reading a piece of fiction.

It is hard to handle. Because it allows you to do almost anything you please, you could lose all discipline and end up with a sprawling mess of a book. You could also struggle to keep your own opinions out of the book, so if you are writing something out of genuine social or political commitment, it could end up sounding like agitprop.

Another form of third-person narration, objective narration, allows us to see only the surface of what's going on — the characters' actions and words. We don't get to go inside anyone's head for their thoughts:

*The woman stirs her tea. There is a cough. She looks up. The man is in the café doorway. He hovers for a moment near her, coughs again, then sits at the neighbouring table. He looks her straight in the face. She turns away, picks up the milk jug again, pours in another drop, all the time continuing to stir. The spoon makes little chinking noises against the rim of the china cup.*

*'It's been hot today,' he says.*

*The woman doesn't respond.*

*The man taps the woman lightly on the shoulder. 'I said, "It's been hot today".'*

With objective narration, the writer's trick is merely to pass on the (seemingly) objective information about what's going on, almost like a fly-on-the-wall documentary might, which is why a great deal of this kind of narrative seems to be in the present tense. The writer's trick is to give the impression of allowing the reader to plug the gaps that are missing, but in reality has chosen very carefully exactly what details to show.

In the right hands, objective narrative can work exceptionally well. You can concentrate on the kind of minute details that somehow say more than the big picture ever will. Handled clumsily, you can end up with something banal and the very fact that we lose the interior lives of the characters we're writing about means that the reader may have to work harder to get to the heart of your story. The eventual story can just lack the warmth and passion that readers tend to want. It works for a novel such as *The Road*, because the whole portrait is bleak and the matter-of-factness of the narrative plays this up.

It's hard to stay entirely objective, though, and even writers such as Cormac McCarthy stray inside the minds of the characters or attribute occasional motives for acts, such as in this snippet from his post-apocalyptic *The Road*:

*The site they picked [to rest] was simply the highest ground they came to and it gave views north along the road and overlooked their backtrack. He spread the tarp in the wet snow and wrapped the boy in the blankets. You're going to be cold, he said. But maybe we won't be here long. Within the hour two men came down the road almost at a lope. When they had passed he stood up to watch them. And when he did they stopped and one of them looked back. He froze. He was wrapped in one of the grey blankets and he would have been hard to see but not impossible. But he thought they had smelled the smoke. They stood talking. Then they went on. He sat down. It's okay, he said. We just have to wait. But I think it's okay.*

## Second person narrators

There are other, less common variations of narrative viewpoint. Occasionally you might find a work of fiction that uses the second person (you). In *Absalom, Absalom!*, William Faulkner uses the second person for some of the narration, one of the most famous passages being:

*You get born and you try this and you don't know why only you keep on trying it and you are born at the same time with a lot of other people, all mixed up with them, like trying to, having to, move your arms and legs with strings only the same strings are hitched to all the other arms and legs and the others all trying and they don't know why either except that the strings are all in one another's way like five or six people all trying to make a rug on the same loom only each one wants to weave his own pattern into the rug; and it can't matter, you know that, or the ones that set up the loom would have arranged things a little better, and yet it must matter because you keep on trying or having to keep on trying and then all of a sudden it's all over.*

This kind of direct address can pull us in as readers; it has a kind of rolling breathlessness about it. But it also has the potential danger that we may feel as if we're being lectured to, being hectored and bullied by the writer, or at the very least being given a gentle lesson. After all, as readers, we come across second-person writing most often in non-fiction, especially instructional/how-to material, such as this very book. It's also slightly distancing. The reader never quite feels as if they're part of the action and so can be very aware that they are reading a piece of fiction.

Unless you feel supremely confident, or use it sparingly in short bursts, it's probably best to leave this kind of writing to highly literary writers.

## First person plural

The same can probably be said of the 1st person plural (we), which seems even rarer than the second person. I'm sure there must be other examples of this, but I know of only two: *The Book of Fame*, by Lloyd Jones and *The Virgin Suicides* by Jeffrey Eugenides. This is from Jones's *The Book of Fame*:

*We woke to English sounds — the scullery, slushing water, roosters, crows, the shuffle of tea trolleys, the song of the washerwoman squeezing her mop at the end of the hall. We lay in our beds, cataloguing these scraps of 'Englishness' for future use. Later we sat up in our beds and pulled back a corner of the curtain to see what was happening down in the street. We could see donkeys with kindling tied to their flanks wobbling down the hill lanes to the market outside the hotel, where thick-ankled women in white pilgrim shawls set down vegetable baskets next to the loaves and round cheeses.*

This is fine writing, but again you run the risk of the reader not being able to cheer on a specific character. This too perhaps should be left to those with the greatest skill, although you could use 'we' occasionally in a first person singular narrative when the narrator is part of a group of people.

## First person

For many new writers, the choice of first person seems a good one. You can pretend to be the main character and develop a voice to suit your narrator. Lodge suggests in *The Art of Fiction* that 'first-person narration appeals to contemporary novelists because it permits the writer to remain within the conventions of realism without claiming the kind of authority which belongs to the authorial narrative methodology of the classic realist novel.' Indeed, first person narrators have a long and worthy history. *Robinson Crusoe* is often seen as the first piece of literature that we could call a novel in the English language. Here is Daniel Defoe writing in the voice of his narrator to describe the clothing he makes for himself:

*I had a short jacket of goat's skin, the skirts coming down to about the middle of the thighs, and a pair of open-kneed breeches of the same; the breeches were made of the skin of an old he-goat, whose hair hung down such a length on either side that, like pantaloons, it reached to the middle of my legs; stockings and shoes I had none, but had made me a pair of somethings, I scarce knew what to call them, like buskins, to flap over my legs, and lace on either side like spatterdashes ...*

Defoe knows that by making it a first-person account, he is making Crusoe's experiences more vivid – he's adding a depth of realism through the notion that this might really be Crusoe himself telling the story. In first person narration, we are often given the impression that what we are reading is genuinely autobiographical. Crusoe's uncertainty over how to describe the clothes he's made harks at the idea that it is an ordinary man telling his tale, rather than a writer with a clever array of vocabulary at his beck and call. Indeed, the full title page of the book as it originally appeared is:

*The Life and Strange Surprising Adventures of Robinson Crusoe, of York, Mariner, who lived eight-and-twenty years, all alone in an uninhabited Island on the Coast of America, near the Mouth of the Great River of Oroonoque; Having been cast on Shore by Shipwreck, wherein all the Men perished but himself. With an Account how he was at last as strangely deliver'd by Pyrates. Written by Himself.*

It may give away a little bit of the plot, but the specific details (Crusoe is from York) and the phrase 'written by himself' do lure us into thinking we've got an early version of one of those misery memoirs. Dickens's *David Copperfield* (which is supposed to be heavily autobiographical anyway) starts with a clear first person narrator:

*Whether I shall turn out to be the hero of my own life, or whether that station will be held by anybody else, these pages must show. To begin my life with the beginning of my life, I record that I was born (as I have been informed and believe) on a Friday, at twelve o'clock at night. It was remarked that the clock began to strike, and I began to cry, simultane-*

*ously.*

*In consideration of the day and hour of my birth, it was declared by the nurse, and by some sage women in the neighbourhood who had taken a lively interest in me several months before there was any possibility of our becoming personally acquainted, first, that I was destined to be unlucky in life; and secondly, that I was privileged to see ghosts and spirits; both these gifts inevitably attaching, as they believed, to all unlucky infants of either gender, born towards the small hours on a Friday night.*

The advantage of first person is that when it is well done, it feels as though the writer is confiding directly in the reader. There's something direct and confessional about it. If we look at J.D. Salinger's famous opening from *The Catcher in the Rye*, which makes reference to Dickens's narrative, we can see how we can use a first person character to establish what is often termed as an unreliable narrator — in other words, one whose words we can't quite trust:

*If you really want to hear about it, the first thing you'll probably want to know is where I was born, and what my lousy childhood was like, and how my parents were occupied and all before they had me, and all that David Copperfield kind of crap, but I don't feel like going into it, if you want to know the truth. In the first place, that stuff bores me, and in the second place, my parents would have about two haemorrhages apiece if I told anything pretty personal about them. They're quite touchy about anything like that, especially my father. They're nice and all — I'm not saying that — but they're also touchy as hell. Besides, I'm not going to tell you my whole goddamn autobiography or anything. I'll just tell you about this madman stuff that happened to me around last Christmas just before I got pretty run-down and had to come out here and take it easy.*

It's almost impossible to imagine this book written in any other way than first person — the narrative voice of Holden Caulfield is what pins us to our seats as we read it. The fact that Caulfield is unaware of the impact of a great many of his words and deeds, or that he can't actually fully understand what is going on around him is part of the novel's great strength. We also see this technique in such works as Kazuo Ishiguro's *The Remains of the Day*, where the butler, Stevens, is so consumed by ideas of duty and dignity that he fails to fully realise that his lord and master has fallen into the lure of Nazism or that he has the chance of true love with the housekeeper, Miss Kenton.

First person can work very well, if you want your narrator to be unreliable — someone whose word we can't quite trust, someone who perhaps doesn't recognise that their world is tilted on a slightly different axis from our own. Holden Caulfield tells us he's not going to give us any David Copperfield crap and then proceeds to give us it all the same. Killers, sociopaths, oddballs, the freaks and the dispossessed will work well in a first person narrative, if you get the tone right, as Iain Banks does with Frank in *The Wasp Factory*:

*I killed little Esmeralda because I felt I owed it to myself and to the world in general. I had, after all, accounted for two male children and thus done womankind something of a statistical favour. If I really had the courage of my convictions, I reasoned, I ought to redress the balance at least slightly. My cousin was simply the easiest and most obvious target.*

*Again, I bore her no personal ill-will. Children aren't real people, in the sense that they are not small males or females but a separate species which will (probably) grow into one or the other in due time. Younger children in particular, before the insidious and evil influence of society and their parents have properly got to them, are sexlessly open and hence perfectly likeable. I did like Esmeralda (even if I thought her name was a bit soppy) and played with her a lot when she came to stay.*

Similarly, Mark Haddon's *The Curious Incident of the Dog in the Night-time* has a teenage protagonist with Asperger's syndrome as its narrator. Christopher Boone finds the dog belonging to his neighbour, Mrs Shears, dead on the front lawn and decides to find out who has killed it. Christopher has huge difficulties understanding human beings and his very literalness means that the way in which he reports what goes on around him is always very matter-of-fact. He also doesn't fully understand what he tells the reader, being unable to understand facial expressions and social nuances. For Christopher, all facts carry equal weight, leaving the reader to pick out the genuinely salient elements of the story:

*Mr. Shears used to be married to Mrs Shears and they lived together until two years ago. Then Mr. Shears left and didn't come back. This was why Mrs Shears came over and did lots of cooking for us after Mother died, because she didn't have to cook for Mr. Shears any more and she didn't have to stay at home and be his wife. And also Father said that she needed company and didn't want to be on her own.*

*And sometimes Mrs Shears stayed overnight at our house and I liked it when she did because she made things tidy and she arranged the jars and pans and tins in order of their height on the shelves in the kitchen and she always made their labels face outwards and she put the knives and forks and spoons in the correct compartments in the cutlery drawer. But she smoked cigarettes and she said lots of things I didn't understand, e.g. 'I'm going to hit the hay,' and 'It's brass monkeys out there,' and, 'Let's rustle up some tucker.' And I didn't like it when she said things like that because I didn't know what she meant.*

*And I don't know why Mr. Shears left Mrs Shears because nobody told me. But when you get married it is because you want to live together and have children, and if you get married in a church you have to promise that you will stay together until death do us part. And if you don't want to live together you have to get divorced and this is because one of you has done sex with somebody else or because you are having arguments and you hate each other and don't want to live in the same house any more and have children. And Mr. Shears didn't want to live in the same house as Mrs Shears any more so he probably hated her and he might have come back and killed her dog to make her sad.*

*I decided to try and find out more about Mr. Shears.*

You can also see the way in which tone is set at the same time as we have an insight into the narrator's character in the start to Albert Camus's The Outsider, where we have a narrator who is both chilling, yet compelling:

*Mother died today. Or maybe yesterday, I don't know. I had a telegram from the home: 'Mother passed away. Funeral tomorrow. Yours sincerely.' That doesn't mean anything. It may have been yesterday.*

There is nothing here about what the central character looks like, but already we are aware that there is something mechanical in his response to the news of his mother's death. Today? Yesterday? Why doesn't that seem to matter to him? Has he no feelings?

James Wood in *How Fiction Works* calls first person narrative, 'a nice hoax: the narrator pretends to speak to us, while in fact the author is writing to us, and we go along with the deception happily enough.' But we can only go along with it to a certain extent. How does your first person narrator speak to us if they are a child, semi-literate or don't have English as their mother tongue?

In his novel, *True History of the Kelly Gang*, Peter Carey's fictionalised version of Ned Kelly is writing his autobiography for his daughter to read when she is old enough:

*All my life all I wanted were a home but I come back from Pentridge Gaol to find the land I had laboured on become a stranger's territory. George King were welcome to it. I didn't care but there was also 30 thoroughbred horses which was my rightful property so when I discovered they was missing I sent word to my mother asking what she done with them. I learned they was stolen and the thief were beyond the law he were Constable Flood of Oxley. That injustice put me in a rage nothing would ease but danger I now craved it like another man might lust for the raw burn of poteen.*

Carey has carefully constructed a voice that tries to capture what an uneducated 19th Century Australian of Irish descent would sound like if he committed his words to paper. This means that there are certain devices and conceits at work in the book. In this particular instance, there are no commas in the novel, but note that Kelly is capable of mastering the apostrophe for possession (stranger's), but not for the omission of letters (didnt). All writing is a con trick, really.

You can also use the first person to narrate a story in which the 'I' character is not the principal player. Dr. Watson does this in the Sherlock Holmes stories. Nick Garraway tells us Jay Gatsby's story. In the main, however, it tends to be less involving than having the first person as the central character, although it does allow the narrative character to boast about how wonderful the main character is.

## Embedded first person

Even where we have a largely third person narration, we can slip in a letter or an email or some other form of writing, which, of course, has to be written in the first person. Casaubon's letter of proposal in *Middlemarch* is a warning sign for what is to come. His prose is tortuous, officious and entirely self-centred. Even when he does get round to complimenting Dorothea Brooke, it is entirely on his own terms:

*My Dear Miss Brooke, I have your guardian's permission to address you on a subject than which I have none more at heart. I am not, I trust, mistaken in the recognition of some deeper correspondence than that of date in the fact that a consciousness of need in my own life had arisen contemporaneously with the possibility of my becoming acquainted with you. For in the first hour of meeting you, I had an impression of your eminent and perhaps exclusive fitness to supply that need (connected, I may say, with such activity of the affections as even the preoccupations of a work too special to be abdicated could not uninterruptedly dissimulate); and each succeeding opportunity for observation has given the impression an added depth by convincing me more emphatically of that fitness which I had preconceived, and thus evoking more decisively those affections to which I have but now referred. Our conversations have, I think, made sufficiently clear to you the tenor of my life and purposes: a tenor unsuited, I am aware, to the commoner order of minds. But I have discerned in you an elevation of thought and a capability of devotedness, which I had hitherto not conceived to be compatible either with the early bloom of youth or with those graces of sex that may be said at once to win and to confer distinction when combined, as they notably are in you, with the mental qualities above indicated. It was, I confess, beyond my hope to meet with this rare combination of elements both solid and attractive, adapted to supply aid in graver labours and to cast a charm over vacant hours; and but for the event of my introduction to you (which, let me again say, I trust not to be superficially coincident with foreshadowing needs, but providentially related thereto as stages towards the completion of a life's plan), I should presumably have gone on to the last without any attempt to lighten my solitariness by a matrimonial union...*

Oh, yes, and there's another lesson to be learned from George Eliot: if you ever receive a marriage proposal that sounds like a solicitor's letter, don't do it.

On a more modern note, Jennifer Egan's *A Visit from the Goon Squad* contains an entire chapter of embedded narrative in the form of a PowerPoint presentation written by a 12-year old.

# A flurry of caveats — first person looks a doddle, but ...

We can see from these extracts that first person narration can be extremely compelling. However, there are huge pitfalls with this point of view.

## It's deceptive

One of the main traps is that it looks far easier than it actually is. After all, we naturally write a great deal of what we do in the first person. Emails, letters, diaries and so forth are almost always first person. It's easy to believe that all you have to do is put yourself in the mind-set of your main character and away you go. It's therefore easy to become too prolix. You're not keeping your narrative tight enough. If you do decide on a first person narrator, you need to keep him or her on a tight rein and be ready to trim plenty of excess fat.

## It often uses just one sense

For some reason, if you write using the first person, there is a tendency to write using just one sense – that of sight. Perhaps this is because everything we get is filtered through the main character's eyes. It's a useful rule, no matter what viewpoint you choose, to involve the other senses – touch, smell, hearing, taste. If you do use these other senses, you'll also find that your writing automatically develops what we might think of as the sixth sense – atmosphere.

## The trap of internal monologue

The trouble is that your narrative character can start to do too much thinking and not enough acting. Yes, this can be the case with third person narrators too, but with first person narrators is so much easier, because you're trying to fully inhabit the skin. It may be the case that you're trying on the voice of the character — that's fine, but too much internal monologue slows everything down. Do we really need to see her hesitate over the choice of paint for the spare room, whether to have latte or cappuccino or which toilet paper is most absorbent?

Robert Graham in his book *The Road to Somewhere* warns us that internal monologue, 'feels claustrophobic and isn't dramatic: no other characters are involved, nobody acts and nobody speaks.' Your main character starts to become reactive, rather than making the story happen.

## Telling instead of showing

When we write in the first person, we more easily find ourselves slipping into telling the reader what's going on, rather than showing them. In some cases, such as the extract from Mark Haddon's *The Curious Incident of the Dog in the Night-time* we have above, it is the actual exposition that becomes compelling, but this is extraordinarily clever writing and perhaps not obvious territory for a beginning writer.

## How do you let the reader know what's going on when your main character's not there?

If we have to filter the story through the first person, we can only see what that person sees. If your protagonist isn't there, how do we get round the problem? You can have another character tell the narrator what's going on, you can use other means of conveying information — the ancient manuscript your hero stumbles upon, letters, emails or other devices. However, there's the danger that there will be an element of artificiality about it, and that we have to have several pages of exposition to catch us up on what the first-person protagonist can't see.

## You can't kill off an 'I' narrator

Well, you can, but it starts getting awkward and potentially unbelievable, unless you're pulling some kind of tricksy narrative, or writing something supernatural. If you're writing any kind of book in which you want to place your main character in genuine danger, if you use a first person voice, we can be pretty sure that he or she isn't going to be mown down before the final page. You've lost the element of jeopardy.

## The tedium of the narrative voice

The reader can get bored with the same narrative voice all the time. In the Peter Carey example we had earlier, some readers might find the awkward grammar and phraseology off-putting after a while. A frequent reaction from book club readers to the kinds of books where there is a strong first-person narrative voice is that readers may not buy into it. Make of that what you will, but it is something to be borne in mind.

## A matter of taste

Some people just don't like it, and not because there's a distinctive voice, but because of lack of one. Fay Weldon is on record as saying that it is 'slack and idle'. And I suspect that if the narrator simply has your voice, your prejudices, your political attitudes and so on, then it can be. She doesn't quite go as far as Henry James, though. He described using the first person as barbaric. So, if you don't want to upset the late Mr. James, then perhaps it's best to think of an alternative.

## Physical description

How do we go about giving a physical description of a first person narrator? Maybe we have to resort to the trick of having them look at themselves in a mirror, but this is a hoary old way of doing it, as Sandra Newman and Howard Mittelmark parody brilliantly in *How Not to Write a Novel*:

*Melinda paused to inspect herself in the mirror. A girl with a nice body and a pretty face stood reflected there, with medium-sized breasts that stood up proudly in her halter top. She gave her long straight cinnamon hair a perky toss and decided Joe would be crazy to let her go.*

When they look in the mirror, most people just check that their tie is straight, or that they haven't got lipstick on their teeth, or their hair is neatly combed. Anyone who spends an excessive amount of time inspecting themselves is probably so egocentric that we wouldn't want to spend a great deal of time in their company.

## Third person narrators

Your third person narrator could be objective, or we can see events close-up through their eyes, almost in the same way as we get a first person narrative. We call this subjective third person (or third person subjective) — where we get inside the skin of the person doing the narration.

There are several advantages to using the third person as the narrator, rather than having a first person narrator. Perhaps most obvious is the fact that you can put your central character into situations of real jeopardy. We don't know for sure if the protagonist will even survive to the end of the book.

We've already seen that you can simulate first person narration by occasionally going inside the head of the narrator. For example, if we take a snippet like this:

*He opened the door slowly and shone the flash-light round the room. What was that? A scurrying, a scuttling, over in the far corner. Rats, probably.*

The question *What was that?* and the fragmentary answer *Rats, probably* come from inside our third person narrator's head. It's immediate and effective. For a quick, highly readable example of the technique, it's worth reading *The Secret Life of Walter Mitty.* Here, James Thurber uses third person, slipping in and out of Mitty's alternative world, a world that exists entirely inside the protagonist's head.

Third person subjective also means that you can manipulate the facts that are placed in front of the reader and win them over to the narrator's point of view. Of course, with third person subjective, you still have the restriction that you need to stay with your narrative character, so if you want the reader to experience things that the narrator possibly can't see for themselves, you've got to find ways round this difficulty.

One simple way is to have more than one third person narrator, which means that you're not then restricted to one point of view. This is sometimes referred to as 'episodically limited' or simply 'episodic'. It's a good way of thinking about longer works. Although again, there are caveats. If we suddenly have three viewpoint characters meet up in a scene, whose viewpoint are we going to go with?

Yes, you can also have several first-person narrators if you want, but you then have to make sure that your different voices are clearly differentiated, which is difficult and even accomplished novelists often struggle to recreate obviously different narrative voices on the page.

If you do decide to use more than one viewpoint character, it's not a bad idea to make that switch obvious, either by giving them separate chapters or clearly delineated sections. In a short story, however, you're probably better off sticking with just one person's viewpoint, no matter which person you choose as your narrator.

## Which to choose first or third?

In most cases, we're likely to use a subjective narrator. But what to choose, third or first person? Perhaps the best way to decide is simply to experiment. Let's imagine that we are going to write a character who is obviously obsessed with a woman he can see from his window. And let's pretend that this is what we've got as a first draft:

*I am your guardian angel.*

> *It is my solemn duty to watch over you.*

> *I need to know your every move.*

> *I need to know every intimate detail of your life, so that when you are not there, I can rehearse your every movement in my mind.*

> *I watch the way you tuck the loose strands of hair when you sit at your desk.*

> *The order in which you set about your work. Laptop lid open, desk-lamp switched on, then back into the shadows of the room.*

What happens if we just change it directly into third person, without much fiddling?

*He is your guardian angel.*

> *It is his solemn duty to watch over you.*

> *He needs to know your every move.*

> *He needs to know every intimate detail of your life, so that when you are not there, he can rehearse your every movement in his mind.*

> *He watches the way you tuck the loose strands of hair when you sit at your desk.*

> *The order in which you set about your work. Laptop lid open, desk-lamp switched on, then back into the shadows of the room.*

It's lost much of its impact by doing this. It's not as claustrophobic or as threatening. If you had a piece that you'd written in the first person, then wanted to change it into third person, then it's not just a simple matter of pressing find/replace and swapping the word "I" with "he" or she" and then tidying up a few subject-verb agreements. We'd probably have to take an entirely different tack. Perhaps we could stay a little on the surface of the narrative, at least to begin with:

*He takes up his position at the bedroom window and looks out across the courtyard to the apartments at the rear of the building.*

*He checks his watch. It's nearly time. The binoculars weigh heavy against his chest. He lifts them to his eyes and focuses in on the wide window above the desk where she is working. He watches her as she goes about her routine. Tucking away the loose strands of hair. Opening the laptop lid. Switching on the desk lamp. Then she moves back into the shadows of the room.*

Again, although this is clunky first draft, we're beginning to get a bit more of a threat into the piece. Changing work from first to third (or vice versa) is therefore more than a simple substitution exercise, it requires a complete overhaul. But as you do, you should get the notion of which you would prefer writing. I suspect that in this case, if it were a novel, I might be tempted to have the creepy voyeur in the first person, no matter what I did with the other focal characters. However, I do think you'd be hard put to sustain that voice across 250-plus pages. Indeed, it would probably lose a great deal of its threatening power.

## Choosing a narrative character

It's not just a question of choosing first or third person. If you're writing a short story and want to stick with one narrative perspective all the way through, you need to decide who your viewpoint character is:

Let's take as an example the following, which is based on a genuine letter to an Agony Aunt, culled from a magazine:

*I'm worried about my daughter, who recently had a baby. She's had problems with depression in the past, so obviously needs a lot of support. My son-in-law complains that I am round at their house too often, but I can't help feeling he's just jealous. He's behaving no better than a spoilt child and I think I should say so.*

Let's imagine that we're going to use this set-up as the basis of a story, but we need to choose which character will be our main narrative character. We have several choices:

1. An over-arching omniscient narrator
2. The mother/mother-in-law, i.e. the author of this letter
3. The daughter/wife
4. The son-in-law/husband/father of the baby
5. The baby
6. Some other character, outside the set-up
7. A mix of the characters

Let's look at all these possibilities in turn:

1. Omniscient narrator. As already mentioned, this can feel a little bit old-fashioned. A narrator who can go in and out of the thoughts of all the people involved means that you lose the possibility of surprising people.

   It might work for a comedy narrative. Jane Austen, for instance, uses it in *Pride and Prejudice*. This means that we already know the nature of a character before we see them in action. However, if we decide that this set-up is only enough material for a short-story, then I suspect that the reader wants to either root for a single character, or see the situation through the eyes of one narrator.
2. The mother/mother-in-law. You may think differently, but I suspect that if we make the mother the narrative character, we need to make her an unreliable narrator (which is what she appears to be in this letter anyway).
3. The daughter/wife. This could be a good choice as she's the character trying to keep everyone happy. It's certainly a good choice if you're aiming for a woman's magazine as you'll have a strong female lead character and a good dilemma to be resolved and character motivation – she probably wants to make everyone happy.
4. The son-in-law/father of the baby. In this letter, he seems to

be very much the villain of the piece. If we chose him, could we play up that villainy and his possible selfishness or should we make him a long-suffering decent chap, hemmed around by feuding women, who finally explodes?

5. The baby. If we choose the baby, we can perhaps get a comic take on all of this. We can have the adults behaving in an entirely babyish way and the baby as the voice of sanity within all this mayhem.

6. Some other character. Yes, we could. We could have a health visitor or one of the husband's relatives. The danger with this, though, is that in a short story, we're dragging in an extra character, who may not add much to the plot.

7. A mix. In a short story, changing viewpoints can often weaken the story we're telling. Perhaps you could get away with two point-of-view characters, but anything more and it might be a little too much chopping and changing.

   Above all, you may find that with whatever you write, you have to experiment before you think you've captured the essence of your narrative character.

## Over to you

Below is another letter to an agony column. It is based on a real example. Imagine you're going to write a 2,000 word story using it as a starting-point.

*For the last couple of years my best friend has had an on-off relationship with her boy-friend. He keeps on finishing it, then comes back a few weeks later. Recently, he actually moved in with her. A couple of nights ago, he went out with a bunch of mates on a lads' night out, but didn't come back and left his mobile switched off. He came strolling back in at lunch-time the next day as if nothing had happened at all. I can't believe she allows him to treat her this way, but she won't have a word said against him. How can I convince her that she's worth more than this and deserves someone better?*

What are the advantages and disadvantages of the following as narrative characters:

- The friend (who writes the letter)
- The girl-friend
- The boy-friend
- More than one narrator
- Someone not mentioned in the letter at all

Who would you choose as the narrative character? Why?

Try a few paragraphs, testing out your choice. Try it in 3$^{rd}$ person and first person. Which do you prefer?

Now write your story.

# 15

# Your character and their world

A character cannot exist in a vacuum. This much is obvious. Any story has to have a setting, so that we can feel rooted in the character's world. That world could be the Roman amphitheatre, a colonised planet in some far-flung galaxy centuries from now, or it could be your home town at the time you're writing.

*The Penguin Dictionary of Literary Terms and literary Theory* defines the word 'setting' as 'the where and when of a story or play; the locale. In drama the term may refer to scenery or props.'

If we say a novel is set in Victorian England, then we're also defining setting in terms of historical period. But a novel set in the dark, satanic mills of Victorian England has a very different setting from one where we only visit the aspidistra-laden drawing-rooms of the upper-middle-classes. 'Setting' also carries with it the notion of milieu and environment.

If we take Miss Haversham out of her crumbling mansion, do we still have Miss Haversham? If you take Heathcliff off the moor is he still Heathcliff? In fact just imagine what *Wuthering Heights* might be like without any of the high ground or the wuthering. If we re-set it in some pleasant Mediterranean village, it loses its fierce rawness.

Setting also helps to create the mood and atmosphere in which your characters will act out their rôles. If we take the classic sitcom *Only Fools and Horses*, the moment Del Boy was financially capable of moving out of the Peckham tower block he shares with too many relatives, Nelson Mandela House, the series became flatter and weaker. The building, the world in which he travelled, the people with whom he socialises – all that is part of what we come to term setting. His character stops resonating with us in the same way when we move him elsewhere. Put money in his pocket and he's robbed of his raison d'être (*This time next year we'll be millionaires*).

Whilst this is a book about character, and not about setting per se, it is hard to separate all these elements, but it is worth bearing in mind that people read books for their settings, possibly just as much as they do for the characters. There are some readers whose diets consist mainly of fantasy or Regency romance or westerns or Scandinavian noir. We've even more recently had the creation of a sub-genre, steam punk, which is a kind of mix of a science fiction future and the machinery of a past era. To its fans, the setting is vital.

Helen Newall suggests that '... part of the pleasure in a text concerns not just the unfolding of events, but the evocation of the environment in which events occur, it's worth spending as much time knowing your setting as you would one of your characters.' Bearing in mind that it's a falsehood to divide up the elements of setting, let's deal with the notions of 'where' and 'when' first, we'll come on to the fictional equivalent of props — a character's possessions — later.

## Place

P. D. James in *Talking about Detective Fiction* says that 'If we believe in the place we can believe in the characters'. Often writers use real places to give a sense of quiddity to their work. Dickens famously used London as a backdrop to everything he wrote. Inspector Morse rarely leaves the dreaming spires of Oxford as one clever body piles up on top of another. Hardy's version of Dorset and the surrounding counties becomes Wessex. You can't separate the works of Thomas Hardy from this largely rural setting. Wessex may not be real, but it is based entirely on reality, which is a clever trick. Taking a place you know, giving it a fictional name and then shaking up what's where is a clever technique. We're often told to write about 'what we know'.

Of course, that place might be entirely fictitious, which gives you as the author the huge advantage of being able to draw your own map. But nonetheless, you're bound to draw on what you know to help create that setting. Science fiction writers can invent entire worlds and planetary systems. Terry Pratchett's *Discworld*, where he parodies all sorts of genres, is famously a disc balanced on the back of four elephants. These elephants in turn stand on the back of a giant turtle. Ludicrous. Next they'll be telling us that we're all clinging onto a lump of rock whirling round a ball of fiery helium.

Aldous Huxley's *Brave New World* gives us a future of sky-scrapers, ultra-cleanliness and stupidly tall buildings. He has a Director of Hatcheries and Conditioning who is in charge of the Neo-Pavlovian conditioning rooms, where babies, genetically honed to fulfil particular jobs will later be used by the Human Element Manager. Everywhere is sanitised and regulated and promiscuity is positively encouraged, even among young children. Although the book dates from 1932, it's wonderfully prescient. Take this short description of a hotel that Lenina and Bernard stay in, just before they go to visit the 'savages' on a reservation:

*The hotel was excellent ... liquid air, television, vibro-vacuum massage, radio, boiling caffeine solution, hot contraceptives, and eight different kinds of scent were laid on in every bedroom. The synthetic music plant was working as they entered the hall and left nothing to be desired. A notice in the lift announced that there were sixty Escalator-Squash-Racquet Courts in the hotel, and that Obstacle and Electro-magnetic Golf could both be played in the park.*

Importantly, the invented world must have its own set of rules. If you can only wear the invisibility cloak during the month of May, then putting it on in June is off-limits. Additionally, if you do create your own world, then you have to do more work to recreate it again in the minds of the reader. You can't get away with just plonking your characters down next to the Eiffel Tower, the Hollywood sign or the Taj Mahal.

## Relating description to your character

It's also a good idea that if you do a set-piece description you both keep it short and also relate that description to your character. Here's a burst of Evelyn Waugh from his novel *Scoop*, where we find William Boot waking up in his eccentric family home, the crumbling Boot Magna Hall:

*An oddly-placed, square window rising shoulder-high from the low wainscot, fringed outside with ivy, brushed by the boughs of a monkey-puzzle; a stretch of faded wallpaper on which hung a water-colour of the village churchyard painted in her more active days by Miss Scope, a small shelf of ill-assorted books and a stuffed ferret, whose death from rat-poisoning had overshadowed the whole of one Easter holiday from his private school — these, according as he woke on his right or left side, greeted William daily at Boot Magna.*

As the pen-as-camera roams around the room, it focuses on William at the end. William is in his natural milieu at Boot Magna Hall and when he goes to London feels ill-at-ease, so when he gets sent by mistake to the African republic of Ishmaelia, he's completely floundering.

Refracting a story's setting through the eyes and ears of a character gives the reader that character's 'take' on the world, much as we saw earlier in the extract from *The Big Sleep* when Philip Marlowe calls at the Sternwood mansion.

## Your character at work

Most of us will spend large parts of our lives earning a crust. Letting someone loose in a working environment can tell us a great deal about a character and gives us several possibilities as writers.

Readers will almost automatically approve of characters who are good at their jobs, especially if that job shows that they look after other people or animals, or that they are especially talented. It's surely no coincidence that so many romances have doctors and nurses as their main characters, as the reader can automatically root for someone who is in a caring profession.

You can also gain empathy for a character if you have them stuck in a job that they don't like. In Keith Waterhouse's novel, *Billy Liar*, Billy Fisher invents a parallel fantasy life to compensate for the dullness of his suburban existence in a dull Yorkshire town. When he arrives at Shadrack and Duxbury's, the firm of undertakers at which he works, we get a flavour of his disaffection and scepticism as he makes the following observations:

*The exterior of Shadrack's, where I now paused to take my traditional deep breath before entering, showed a conflict of personalities between young Shadrack and Old Duxbury, the two partners. Young Shadrack, taking advantage of Duxbury's only trip abroad, a reciprocal visit by the town council to Lyons ... had pulled out the Dickensian windows, bottle-glass and all, and substituted modern plate-glass and a shop sign of raised stainless-steel lettering. Thus another piece of old Stradhoughton bit the dust and the new effect was of a chip shop on a suburban housing estate.* [In the window was a sign ...] *and a piece of purple cloth on which there was deposited a white vase, the shape of a lead weight, inscribed to the memory of a certain Josiah Olroyd. The reason Josiah Olroyd's vase was in Shadrack's window and not in the corporation cemetery was that his name had been misspelled, and the family had not unreasonably refused to accept the goods.*

A description such as this tells us not only about the narrative character, but also gives us his views on a whole range of topics, not least the two men he works for. We also get a snapshot of small-town civic life.

The minutiae of different jobs can also help towards character-isation. What is it really like to be a nurse, fire-fighter or a teacher in an inner-city school? Can you, as the writer, go and experience some of these things for yourself in order to add textual details and richness to the environment in which your characters operate?

## Period settings

All work dates. If you set your story in the present, a few years down the line, it will automatically be in the past. However, this need not worry you too much. Whilst we may not understand get all the social nuances of George and Weedon Grossmiths' *Diary of a Nobody*, we still see Charles Pooters around us to this day. The importance he attaches to his suburban house does not date. Nor does his buying of status symbols on the never-never. Look down any aspirant suburban road today and you'll see sleek 4x4s and can be pretty sure that few of them have been bought outright. In the late 1880s, owning a piano was more-or-less the equivalent:

*There is always something to be done: a tin-tack here, a Venetian blind to put straight, a fan to nail up, or part of a carpet to nail down all of which I can do with a pipe in my mouth; while Carrie is not above putting a button on a shirt, mending a pillow-case, or practising the 'Sylvia Gavotte' on our new cottage piano (on the three years' system), manufactured by W. Bilkson (in small letters), from Collard and Collard (in very large letters).*

The advantage of setting your work now is that there is probably far less research to be done. The Grossmiths probably needed only to wander down any terrace in Holloway to find a house just like 'The Laurels'. You may want to research a specific place, but the general Zeitgeist is almost bound to seep into what you write.

It's much harder setting your work in the past. You have to get it right as there is always somebody who knows better than you do. I once had a stage-play set in the 1870s, in which one of the working-class characters tries to open a window on the train, only to be roundly informed that the trains running on that particular line only had opening windows in First Class. Yes, I too felt that this critic really needed to get out more or develop a taste for hospital food. But, in a needling, annoying way, they were right. Something I was working on recently involved the use of the Bic plastic lighter, not invented until five years after my protagonist used it, so we had to go back to a box of matches. Getting some detail wrong is like holing a boat below the water-line. If the writer's made a mistake with that little detail, how can I trust them? Are other things incorrect?

Of course, the Internet is a boon for researchers, but you can actually suffer from the problem of researching too much. Once you have collected every tiny detail, it has to be shoe-horned into your writing no matter what. I once heard a writer of historical fiction say that she did her research afterwards. There's possibly something to be said for that. You can find out how much the armour weighed, or the foreman was paid, or what they had for breakfast in Wandsworth Gaol afterwards. It also stops you doing what is so easy to do and that is searching on the net and then finding two hours later that you've forgotten what you were looking for, but are now expert on the mating habits of the Ecuadorian mango fly.

In Hilary Mantel's novel, *Wolf Hall*, Cardinal Wolsey has fallen out of favour. He is about to be evicted from his house, York Place, by King Henry VIII, who is going to install Anne Boleyn there. Wolsey has been extraordinarily extravagant. In this extract, a posse arrives to strip the place both to enrich the king and to get it ready for re-modelling. The process takes up several pages, but here's a taste:

*They are overturning chests and tipping out their contents. They scatter across the floor, letters from Popes, letters from the scholars of Europe: from Utrecht, from Paris, from Santiago de Compostela; from Erfurt, from Strassburg, from Rome. They are packing his gospels and taking them for the king's libraries. The texts are heavy to hold in the arms, and awkward as if they breathed; their pages are made of slunk vellum from stillborn claves, reveined by the illuminator in tints of lapis and lead-green...*

*In the two great rooms that adjoin the gallery, they have set up trestle tables. Each trestle is twenty feet long and they are bringing up more. In the Gilt Chamber they have laid out the cardinal's gold plate, his jewels and precious stones, and they are deciphering his inventories, and calling out the weight of the plate...*

Not only is the novel thoroughly researched, but the detail enables us to sink fully into the period. It's also more than a physical description of what's going on, but gives us a picture both of the man who is going to lose all this, and the kind of man who is prepared to strip out a house and make it over for his mistress. Note that even tiny details like the spelling of Strasburg as Strassburg add to the sense of our understanding of the time, and, of course, the place. That detail about the vellum from stillborn calves is a killer. It's the kind of nugget that any writer of historical fiction would love to unearth, yet it is slipped in almost in passing.

## Characterisation through possessions

*Jim Tough glanced at his Rolex Oyster watch. He was going to be late for the cocktail party. He rammed in the clutch on his Ferrari Testarossa and changed gears. It was a hot day and his Savile Row suit was beginning to feel a little bit more crumpled than it should do, given the money he'd paid for it (he'd put the bill on his Amex Platinum Club Card). The needle jumped above 90. That was better. He could picture Jasmine, waiting by the pool of their mansion. He hoped Fortnum and Mason had delivered the seventeen hampers he'd ordered and that the*

*Dom Perignon was already on ice.*

Possessions are another aspect of the milieu a character inhabits. Choosing them carefully, helps to embed that character in the world you are creating.

But the passage we've got above is revolting. This is a sad case of the author thinking that by simply listing what Jim Tough owns, you have created a character. You haven't. It's an easy trap to fall into that by giving us a list of labels, you've somehow given us a portrait of a person.

That's not to say that some brands won't carry a certain weight. If you give a character a brand of cigarettes to smoke, that indicates something. You wouldn't give a hard-drinking, hard-swearing roustabout mentholated cigarettes. Smokers of Consulate are very different to people who smoke Capstan Full Strength. Sobranie Cocktail cigarettes are not the staple smoke of blue-collar workers, nor would a 1950s debutante be hand-rolling her cigarettes, unless it were to include some banned substance or as a deliberate attempt to seem part of an alternative scene to alienate her horrified parents.

It's very easy to get something very wrong. The wealthiest people I know don't give a stuff about where they buy anything, except that what they do buy is good. When they buy wine, they aren't attracted by the label, but take the car over to France, tour a few less well-known vineyards and come back with wine that most of us will have never heard of at supermarket prices. They don't wear Rolex watches, possibly for a couple of reasons. The first is that it's probably a sign of being *nouveau riche*, the second is that they're entirely happy that a watch should just tell them the time. I know someone with oodles of money who typically buys a new watch every time the local petrol station allows you to collect tokens to save towards one.

I was working with a group of university students a while back and asked them if they thought a living-room with a three-piece suite was an indication of a room being high-class or not. Most of them felt that it was. Yet, stick a matching sofa and easy chairs set under the nose of the gentry and they would be horrified. No, matching furniture is a sign of aspiring to something. People with real, inherited money don't need to aspire to anything at all and make do with whatever comes their way, handed down the generations, and possibly made by Hepplewhite or Chippendale. As Alan Clarke once said about Michael Heseltine, 'He's the kind of man who has to buy his own furniture.'

For a fine example of using possessions to create character, then the short story *The Things That They Carried* is hard to beat. It's one of those stories that deceives you with its simplicity. O'Brien characterises the various members of a platoon by the objects they haul around in their rucksacks through the jungles of Vietnam. He progresses the story of a lieutenant hardening up as one of the soldiers in his platoon is killed by a sniper.

*They carried USO* [United Service Organisation] *stationery and pencils and pens. They carried Sterno* [cooking fuel], *safety pins, trip flares, signal flares, spools of wire, razor blades, chewing tobacco, liberated joss sticks and statuettes of the smiling Buddha, candles, grease pencils,* **The Stars and Stripes***, fingernail clippers, Psy Ops* [Psychological Operations] *leaflets, bush hats, bolos, and much more. Twice a week, when the resupply choppers came in, they had hot chow in green Mermite cans and large canvas bags filled with iced beer and soda pop. They carried plastic water containers, each with a two-gallon capacity. Mitchell Sanders carried a set of starched tiger fatigues for special occasions. Henry Dobbins carried Black Flag insecticide. Dave Jensen carried empty sandbags that could be filled at night for added protection. Lee Strunk carried tanning lotion. Some things they carried in common. Taking turns, they carried the big PRC-77 scrambler radio, which weighed thirty pounds with its battery.*

Pulling a snippet of the story out of context doesn't give the full flavour as O'Brien mixes not just tangible items, such as weaponry, clothing, photographs or tanning lotion, but also the notion that people carry memories, fears and hopes. It's the mix of the factual, from the mundane to the bizarre (tanning lotion in a war?), together with the emotions that make this such a powerful story.

In a way, James Thurber does something similar, with his main character in *The Secret Life of Walter Mitty*, another frequently anthologised story. Thurber's take is comic, rather than serious, though. Mitty is brought out of his reveries by his wife's demands that he buy overshoes. Overshoes (galoshes) are surely a sign of timidity – they're for someone who can't even get their shoes dirty. Mitty dreams he is captain of a hydroplane, a resourceful surgeon, a sharp shooter on trial, a fighter pilot and about to face a firing squad with a cigarette dangling jauntily from the corner of his mouth, but he still gets into trouble from his wife for not putting on his galoshes in the shop. There are plenty of other mundane things that Thurber could have given Mitty to buy, but choosing overshoes underlines Mitty's meekness.

## Over to you
1. Your character's possessions.

- What is in your protagonist's handbag or wallet and pockets?
- What clothes are in his/her wardrobe?
- If you open their fridge, what's on the shelves?
- Write a shopping list for your character.

2. The world of work. Where does your character work? What are the sights, smells and sounds of their working environment? Do they have their own desk, locker, office

or workstation? Have they personalised this area in any way? What's in the filing-cabinet or the desk-drawer? Do they steal anything from work? Where do they eat their lunch? Where do they make themselves a drink? If your character were summarily sacked and had to put all their personal items in a cardboard box, would they fit? What would be in that box?

3. The world around you. Take a sheet of paper and divide it into five sections, one for each of the senses: sight, sound, touch, smell, taste.

   Now go outside your house and take a trip down the road where you live. Jot down what you encounter under each of these headings.

   Once you're back home, have a character make the same journey you've just made, but have them react to their surroundings. Perhaps they love it, perhaps they hate it. Perhaps they've arrived from another planet and are trying to get their head (if they have one) around what's taking place on planet earth.

# 16

## A rose by any other name

Whenever any of my writing classes starts to discuss character names, I always warn them that we're bound to tread on someone's corns. The name that has you clasping your hand over your mouth to silence your giggles is the one that someone else's new darling grandchild has just been given.

We all come to names with a set of preconceived ideas. I've always imagined that any girl called Nigella or Michaela was probably the first-born child of a Nigel or a Michael, who would have to live with the disappointment that his wife produced a daughter for the rest of his life. You'll have your own pet prejudices too.

Additionally, all of these hang-ups and foibles are reinforced by what we find in life. When school-teachers come to name their own children, they always have a fund of anecdotes as to why they can't call them something fairly straightforward. They had a Jennifer who bullied the other kids. There was a David who used to pick his nose and wipe it under the chair. And what William did is so completely unmentionable that, given you might be eating a sandwich whilst reading this, I won't.

Years ago, when I was a school-teacher, we used to joke that we could tell how well-behaved a class was likely to be, just by looking at the register. If you had too many Jasons, Lees, Karens, Samanthas and Kevins you'd know you'd got your work cut out. If there were any Darrens or Charlenes, you'd try to find someone to swap classes. In fact, there was a survey done a few years ago that bore this staffroom joke out. Nowadays, it's the Calums, Connors, Aleishas and Courtneys who are subject to teacher preconceptions.

In 1933, the name Adolf suddenly rose in popularity, when

Germany elected a new leader. It's now almost impossible to find any German boy with the name, and one does suspect that any who are given it will be the child of neo-Nazis. Giving a character the name Adolf is tricky as there is such an immediate association. Other names that almost preclude usage because of either real-life or their high-profile usage in a book or film might include Humbert, Myra, Barack, Hyacinth or Hilda. For years after the film *The Omen* came out, you'd have been hard-pressed to find anyone who was prepared to call their son Damien.

Through a mixture of both sound reasoning and our silly prejudices, previous experiences and foibles, names have a huge resonance and what we call our characters is vitally important. As Rosemary Aitken says in *Writing a Novel – A Practical Guide*, 'names have been demonstrated to set up assumptions … and no matter how irrational that is, it is helpful to the novel writer to be aware of this'.

Writers have realised the importance of names for centuries. John Bunyan's *The Pilgrim's Progress*, which to most modern tastes is heavy-handed and didactic, has a central character called Christian. Christian is an everyman figure (and I do mean everyman, not everywoman), who sets out to save himself from sin. The characters he meets on his journey have names such as Helpful, Faithful, Giant Despair, Ignorance, Mercy, Evangelist and Pliable. No guesses as to what they represent. *The Pilgrim's Progress* doesn't go in for subtlety when it comes to names (or moral lessons).

We may feel that this is a bit obvious for clever 21st Century readers, but Martin Amis's novel *Money*, pillorying the acquisitiveness and solipsism of Thatcher's Britain, has John Self as its protagonist. In J. K. Rowling's *Harry Potter* series, we have bold naming in Voldermort, Ron Weasley, Sirius Black and Hagrid amongst others. These are echoes of Charles Dickens, who also gave his characters colourful names — Charity and Mercy Pecksniff, Tilly Slowboy, Wackford Squeers. Indeed only slightly cleverer variations exist in many modern books. Surely Hannibal Lecter is only so named to give us the rhyming epithet Hannibal the Cannibal?

I suspect that we live with all these fairly obvious choices, because they work in favour of the character. Calling your flesh-eating serial killer with a high IQ and refined tastes (and not just in human flesh) Hannibal just to get in the rhyme might be a bit obvious, but it works. And it's possibly better than calling him Brian. With apologies to any Brians reading this: yes, you can have a serial killer with your name, but he will be a more low-key villain. It will be his ordinariness that will work for him, not the fact that he is exceptional and clever, as is the case with Hannibal. Brian the serial killer is much more likely to be a quiet chap, perhaps with a record of overdue library fines and the inability to form relationships, especially with women. He may spend more time than is strictly necessary in his shed. Apologies again, Brians.

Naming a character wrongly is almost bound to work against you, but choosing the right name can be a bonus. Even before we know anything else about a character, we may know a great deal just from their name. Names automatically bring with them assumptions about age, social class and educational level. They are fundamental to the character-building process.

## Your character's age

Names denote age. Even those names that seem never to drop out of fashion can be played with to help the reader identify how old a character is. You can call your heroine Elizabeth, and she could be anything from a young girl to an elderly lady. But what about its variations? A Betty is not a Bet and a Liz is not the same as a Lizzie, or for that matter a Beth, Bess, Elsie, Eliza, Liza, Bessie, or any other variation you can bring to mind. A Lizzie, for instance, sounds as though she will be younger than a Betty. To my ears, a Betty will always be an older woman, as would a

Dorothy. Just about everyone of my generation had an Auntie Dorothy; in fact, it might have been illegal not to. At the time of writing, the name seems to have dropped out of fashion, but call a character Dorothy or Edith or Ethel and we already have a decent idea what kind of age they are, as well as other aspects of their personality. A Frederick might be a Fred or a Freddy. A James might a Jim, a Jimmy, a Jamie or a Jimbo. They will all be very different from one another.

## Class and names

In Britain, we're obsessed with class differences, no matter how much we pretend otherwise. Jilly Cooper's romping toff is called Rupert Edward Algernon Campbell-Black. What better name for the caddish bounder of light-hearted page-turners? The name might not work for something a bit more serious, but Jilly Cooper knows how to belt out a tale and slightly larger-than-life names do the job excellently. Any fictional character called Rupert, let's face it, is almost bound to belong to the squirearchy. Or wear loud checked trousers.

What do you know about a Trevor, a Kevin, a Marmaduke, a Simeon or a Tristram before they've even opened their mouths? Is a Marcus from further up society's ladder than a Mark? Where on that ladder would you find Crispin, Gideon, Rufus, Camilla, Aurora, Melissa, Margot, Lucinda, Francesca or Henrietta? Where does a Kylie, a Petronella, a Cynthia, a Doris or a Doreen buy her clothes? Surely, you won't find them shopping in the same place? Who will be buying clothes at Oxfam? Who will be unhappy if there isn't a smart label inside (or outside) their skimpy top? Who will be having their clothes tailor-made by a couturier? Does a Britney have more tattoos than a Bella?

Names tell us something about parents. You've had my ideas on Michaela and Nigella, but does a mother call her daughter Cressida because she's a Shakespeare junkie or Isadora after Isadora Duncan, because she liked the film with Vanessa

Redgrave? Let's not forget the Johnny Cash song about the boy deliberately given the name Sue just to toughen him up.

## Names for historical characters

If naming modern characters is tricky enough, then anyone who has ever researched their family tree must have encountered the difficulty that if we drop back a hundred or more years in time, families had the habit of persisting with a small number of names. You can easily find that the first-born son of each generation is called James or Joseph. Not only that, but sometimes the child dies in infancy and the parents re-use the name for another child born later on.

When you're writing historical fiction, you have a smaller pallet of names to draw on. A novel set in Georgian England restricts you to biblical names or those of Kings and Queens. Call your 1829 scullery maid Kayleigh and you've essentially blown yourself out of the water. Wandering graveyards is a good place to look for historical names, as is reading literature of the period. You still have the luxury of choosing almost any surname you like. You may even find one in your family tree. My wife has a Samson Warrilow in hers. I have an ancestor with the forename Micah.

## Names from a different culture or country

If we're going to write about countries or cultures different to our own, then we have to understand the subtleties. Every now and then I get lovely little email messages inviting me to help gentlemen move money that has been trapped in a bank in some central African dictatorship. Often these implausible invitations have some vaguely westernised name attached to them, so you might find they've been sent by someone as unlikely as Christian Goldblatt or Asif Simpson. Alternatively, they pick on something so ultra-ordinary that this too rouses suspicion — John Smith, Fred Brown, Jane Evans.

Somehow the names just don't ring true. Unless you are immersed in another culture, this can be problematic, for the very reasons we're exploring here. You may have no idea what the resonances are. Even within the context of the British Isles, we have names that are going to differ from one country to the next. John will find himself Sean, Ian, Evan or Ivan in various Celtic forms. Maeve, Finola and Eamonn are likely to be Irish. Campbell, Maxwell, Morag, Fergus and Fiona are probably Scottish. Sian, Angharad, Dewi and Gareth are all names we would associate with Wales. You'd be making a poor choice if you were to call your supporter of the English national football team Llewellyn Rees (although Emlyn Hughes did captain the England football team, but that's real life, not fiction).

## Ironic names

Irony is useful in non-comic writing, but comes into its own in comedy. In the classic sitcom *One Foot in the Grave*, the main character is called Victor. He's anything but a Victor as life doles out a series of minor defeats. You might choose to call a sexually-frustrated character Roger, a deceitful liar Frank, a foot-stamping virago Patience. Perhaps the aforesaid Samson Warrilow was an eight-stone weakling. Or bald.

## Ambivalent names

It's probably best to avoid giving a character one of those names that is used by either sex. Evelyn Waugh's first wife was also called Evelyn, which may have save a fortune on the cost of printing the letter-headed paper, but it must also have been extremely difficult to split up their book collection when they divorced. ('That's my book.' 'No, it's not, it's got my name in the front.' 'No, that's my name.') Hilary, Jocelyn and Leslie/Lesley are probably also worth avoiding. I shouldn't have to tell you that the story in which your character Sam, Chris or Charlie turns out to be a woman after all and not the man they expected should be binned straight away. Sorry.

## Villains and other nasty people

A good villain deserves a good name. According to the story, Ian Fleming was at school with the brother of Henry Blofeld, the cheery cricket commentator. No guesses at to where he got the surname of one of his villains from, then. But Bond books date from a different era and, during the Cold War, it was enough to give characters East German or Soviet-sounding names to make them sound evil, although the bilabial stop at the end of the name Rosa Klebb is chilling whatever the context. We may want our villains' names to be a little bit more subtle than Ian Fleming's Auric Goldfinger or J. K. Rowling's Voldemort.

But there are some tricks that work every time, and are not necessarily obvious to the reader. S- sounds are good for the names of unpleasant characters. Sn- sounds are even better and Sl- sounds probably top the bill. Perhaps it's because so many words starting with sn- or sl- have unpleasant connotations: slithering, slimy, sleazy, sloppy, slobbering, slippery, snobbish, sniffing, snot, slavering... Treat your protagonist to an enemy called Snape or Snetterton or Slaven or Slyfield.

## What do your characters call one another?

In our lives, we are known by different names to different people. You may be Mum to your children, Mrs. Jones when you go to the hospital, Rebecca when your mother phones you up, Becks to your old school mates and only your husband calls you Becky. In the same way in fiction, you can help establish the various relationships between your characters. As an obvious example of how relationships are changed by the use of names, Homer Simpson's son, Bart, calls him Homer rather than Dad, thus underscoring the fact that Bart doesn't always hold his father in the highest esteem.

# Finding names when you're stuck

## Neutral names

If names carry such resonances, it's often hard to get a character name right before you start out. If you can't think of a name immediately for a character, but you want to press on with your writing, then here's a little tip. Instead of forcing a name that doesn't work on a character, just give them what seems like a neutral name to you. For me, these are names such as Peter, John, Susan, Mary, Anne, Sarah. You will have your own 'neutral' names, I'm sure. When the character establishes itself, then you can choose something appropriate.

## Phonebooks and other annual publications

As well as graveyards, the phonebook – or indeed any gazetteer – is a great place to find names. However, instead of lifting a name wholesale from the book, try putting together a first name and a surname from different pages. This will also help you avoid the looming spectre of libel.

Above all, remember that your character's name is of vital importance. It carries far more weight for the reader than you might expect.

## Over to you

1. Assuming you're working on a story right now, have you chosen a name for your main character? How do other characters refer to your protagonist? Do they have particular shortened versions of that name? Or some other name altogether?
2. What is the difference between an Edward, an Ed, an Eddie and a Teddy?
3. You come across the name Genevieve. If you were going to create character with that name, what kind of person would she be?

4. Think of a suitable name for the following obvious types
   — you might even like to think of one name for a serious,
   more contemplative piece of writing and one for a
   comedy:

- A put-upon man who is unhappy both at home and at
  work, but who can't seem to say 'no' to anyone who wants
  him to do something for them. Underneath it all, he
  resents what is taking place, but always feels morally
  bound to be obliging and helpful.
- A woman who is at war with her neighbours over the
  tiniest, silliest little detail. Their car is parked in slightly
  the wrong place, they've planted a shrub that gives her
  hay-fever, the kids have kicked a ball into her garden for
  the umpteenth time this week.
- A school-teacher who cannot keep order in the classroom.

# 17

# The villain of the piece

If we were to be a bit more subtle in the title heading here, perhaps we should have used the word 'antagonist' or 'opponent'. The word 'villain' conjures up the image of a cat-stroking evil-genius or some Victorian squire twirling his moustaches, 'Now that's as fine a piece of flesh as I've seen without a saddle ...'

Villains come in all shapes and sizes. Many of us will have our favourites: Wackford Squeers, Bill Sykes, Cruella de Vil, The Wicked Witch of the West, Alec D'Urbeville, Professor Moriarty, Mrs Danvers, Count Dracula or Ernst Stavro Blofeld. We might even enjoy our great villainous anti-heroes, such as Patricia Highsmith's wonderfully amoral Tom Ripley or Pinkie Brown from *Brighton Rock*.

Whilst we will deal with villains in the old-fashioned sense of the word here, bear in mind that we're also talking about antagonists — people who oppose your protagonist, or get in their way. These people may not be villains as such, but it is from their negative characteristics that they gain their impetus.

'Give your protagonist worthy opponents' is the dictum. James Bond can't save the world unless he is faced with a villain who is ready to blow it up. If all he had lined up against him was some minor crook, hoping to knock off the cash-register from the all-night petrol station, then where would be the fun in that? No, he needs megalomaniacs, psychopaths and deviants bent on world domination.

The world of James Bond tends to be a tad larger than life and we may be aiming for something more subtle, but the truth is that unless our protagonists have got someone difficult standing in the way of their goal, then there's really no story.

## Villainous villains

Let's start with villainous villains. Really nasty, evil ones, ones that you wouldn't like to meet in full sunshine, let alone a darkened alley-way.

We've looked at the technique of mentioning characters so that we know something about them before we get to see them in action. We saw how Jay Gatsby had a big build up with people discussing his past before appearing in *The Great Gatsby*. The building of reputation before we meet the villain is a staple technique. It's one that Conan Doyle understood. In *The Final Problem*, when Dr. Watson confesses that he has never heard of Professor Moriarty, Holmes fills him in:

*'He is the Napoleon of crime, Watson. He is the organiser of half that is evil and of nearly all that is undetected in this great city. He is a genius, a philosopher, an abstract thinker. He has a brain of the first order. He sits motionless, like a spider at the centre of its web, but that web has a thousand radiations, and he knows well every quiver of each of them. He does little himself. He only plans. But his agents are numerous and splendidly organized. Is there a crime to be done, a paper to be abstracted, we will say a house to be rifled, a man to be removed – the word is passed to the Professor, the matter is organized and carried out. The agent may be caught. In that case money is found for his bail or his defence. But the central power which uses the agent is never caught – never so much as suspected. This was the organisation which I deduced, Watson, and which I devoted my whole energy to exposing and breaking up.*

*'But the professor was fenced round with safeguards so cunningly devised that, do what I would, it seemed impossible to get evidence which would convict in a court of law...'*

Of course, a man as clever as Sherlock Holmes has to have a criminal mastermind for a nemesis. And whilst the idea of the evil genius may be a little clichéd now, there are some subtleties to be noted about Moriarty. Not least that he doesn't commit the crimes himself. Whilst Holmes is perfectly willing to roll up his sleeves, Moriarty does everything at arm's length, making the reader see him as both manipulative and effete. Even before Moriarty has done anything at all, we know a great deal about him.

Thomas Harris also pulls off something of the same trick in *The Silence of the Lambs*. Although Hannibal Lecter does appear in a previous book, *The Silence of the Lambs* is expected to work as a stand-alone book in its own right, so Lecter is given a big build-up. In FBI Section Chief Jack Crawford's office, Crawford tells Clarice Starling that they've been interviewing serial killers to build up profiles:

*'...But the one we want the most, we haven't been able to get. I want you to go after him tomorrow in the asylum.'*

*Clarice Starling felt a glad knocking in her chest and some appre-hension too.*

*'Who's the subject?'*

*'The psychiatrist — Dr. Hannibal Lecter,' Crawford said.*

*A brief silence follows the name, always, in any civilised gathering.*

Harris takes a good deal of time to have our characters provide us not just with a portrait of Lecter, but by extension, of Clarice Starling and Jack Crawford. Starling eventually arrives at the psychiatric hospital in which Lecter is held and meets with the unpleasant director of the facility, Dr. Chilton. After giving us various bits on information about Lecter, including the fact he probably hasn't seen a woman in years and that he writes learned articles for scientific journals, Chilton begins reciting the rules about meeting Hannibal Lecter:

*'...Do not reach through the bars, do not touch the bars. You pass him nothing but soft paper. No pens, no pencils... The paper you pass him*

*must be free of staples, paper clips, or pins. Items come back out through the sliding food carrier. No exceptions. Do not accept anything he attempts to hold out to you through the barrier...*

*'Lecter is never outside his cell without wearing full restraints and a mouthpiece... I'm going to show you why ... On the afternoon of July 8, 1976, he complained of chest pain and was taken to the dispensary. His restraints were removed to make it easier to give him an electrocardiogram. When the nurse bent over him, he did this to her.' Chilton handed Clarice Starling a dog-eared photograph. 'The doctors managed to save one of her eyes. Lecter was hooked up to the monitors the entire time. He broke her jaw to get at her tongue. His pulse never got over eighty-five, even when he swallowed it.'*

All this before we set eyes on Dr. Lecter. Harris doesn't even attempt to describe the photograph Chilton passes Starling; he just lets us see her reaction and, intriguingly, Chilton's reaction to hers. By the time poor Clarice Starling walks down the corridor to Lecter's cell, we know that she is dealing with someone almost super-human. Then, when we do meet him, we know he's the kind of person who maintains full eye contact when it suits him.

*Dr Lecter's eyes are maroon and they reflect the light in pinpoints of red. Sometimes the points of light seem to fly like sparks to his centre. His eyes held Starling whole.*

Not many people in fiction have maroon eyes, and no matter how unlikely we think it might be, somehow it seems to work. But the great thing about Hannibal Lecter, just as with Iago in Shakespeare's *Othello*, is that there seems to be no overall motive for his actions. We have no idea why Dr. Lecter enjoys human flesh. We have no idea why Iago wants to bring down Othello. We know they want to do these things – the characters have clear goals, but we don't have any indication of the reasons why they want what they want. You may disagree, but for me this makes them much stronger, more unpredictable than giving some weak Freudian explanation for their behaviour. It also means that you can't stop the bad behaviour by addressing the cause of it, because there doesn't seem to be a cause.

Clever (in their own way), inventive criminals make good villains. If our protagonists are up against sloppy lazy criminals with records as long as your arm who leave DNA and finger-prints all over the crime scene and have their mail forwarded to their new address, then where's the challenge? You can be a successful burglar or you can be known to the police.

If we look back to where we used the science of psychology to help us think about characters and the Hare test for Psychopathy (Hare PCL-R), we can easily come up with a list of the kinds of attributes that make villains villainous. Whilst the average serial rapist or killer is likely to be a psychopath, not all psychopaths are rapists and killers. In fact, you're far more likely to find them in the boardroom, managing the sales force or, surprisingly enough, amongst the clergy than you are in a back alley with a carving knife.

Psychopaths are manipulative. They are likely to take enjoyment from other people's misery. Their relationships with other people are entirely superficial. They will show as much friendliness as they need in order to get what they want. And what they want is normally power and prestige, which is perhaps why one estimate suggests that business leaders are four times more likely to be psychopaths. God forbid that any should end up in parliament.

A psychopath will have no remorse for what they do, because they have no conscience. Whilst they may be able to put on a front that will deceive people, underneath it, there is nothing but naked self-interest. Perhaps Iago and Lecter are both psychopaths.

If you stick your psychopath in the workplace, they will stay incredibly cool under pressure, but will be far more interested in climbing the corporate ladder than in the welfare of anyone at work. This extends to their taking the credit for anything, regardless of whether they did it or not. If you want to set a villain loose in the workplace, having them pretend that they were the one who sewed up the multi-million pound deal when it was our protagonist, in fact, who did it, is as good a way of making life tough for you hero or heroine.

In his book, *Galapagos*, one of Kurt Vonnegut's central characters is a psychopath, Andrew MacIntosh. MacIntosh isn't some axe-wielding maniac, but here are some of the things that Vonnegut's narrator says about him after he appears on a TV show, talking about 'The Nature Cruise of the Century', a specialist boat trip to visit the Galapagos islands, where MacIntosh has spoken out about the need for conservation:

*It is a joke to me that this man should have presented himself as an ardent conservationist, since so many of the companies he served as a director or in which he was a major stockholder were notorious damagers of the water or the soil or the atmosphere. But it wasn't a joke to MacIntosh, who had come into this world incapable of caring much about anything. So, in order to hide this deficiency, he had become a great actor, pretending even to himself that he cared about all sorts of things...*

*...Like so many other pathological personalities in power a million years ago, he might do almost anything on impulse, feeling nothing much. The logical explanations for his actions, invented at leisure, always came afterwards...*

*... Like most pathological personalities, Andrew MacIntosh never cared much whether what he said was true or not — and so he was tremendously persuasive.*

## Less villainous villains — the flawed character
There is, however, a more subtle kind of villain, one whose villainy stems not from some kind of sociopathic evil, but

because, like all of us, this person has some character flaw. Perhaps rather than seeing them as villains, we should think of them as unsympathetic characters. If we only have 'good' characters, then we have nothing to rub up against. In Commedia dell'Arte the servant girl Columbina is the straight rôle, the one who provides us with a sensible, moral compass by which we can judge the silliness of the behaviour of other characters. Conversely, even in the pleasantest and gentlest of tales, we need some kind of 'enemy' for our protagonist. These are the ones who will obstruct our protagonist, or make their lives more uncomfortable.

We don't have to travel very far to see the kind of behaviour that will make a character less sympathetic to the reader. We probably all know someone who is materialistic. If a friend comes round, showing off the latest car, these people also have to have such a vehicle, but with the added embellishment of a personalised number-plate or a bigger satnav screen. They are the kind of people who tend to judge both their own self-worth and those of the people around them by their possessions. It's a fairly hollow attitude. It's the 'I don't get out of bed for less than ...' syndrome that places a financial value on everything they do and everything they possess.

Now, most of us probably have a shade of materialism in our souls (I bet you've got hundreds of books). So let's not get too snotty about this. The point at we get too judgemental about our villains, is probably the moment at which they become caricatures. Indeed, it's worth remembering this piece of advice from Nicholas Shakespeare (quoted in Roberts, Mitchell & Zubrinch's *Writers on Writing*):

*Fiction demands that you share a cigarette with your enemy, that you look him in the eye before you shoot, that you see him in all the roundness, that you don't judge him ... in a novel, if you judge the character, it decays the character ... in a sense you must be in love with them all, or you must be compassionate or at least empathetic with them all.*

If we do have a character who likes gadgets, gizmos and shiny cars, we can't sit in judgement on them, feeling morally superior; we also have to understand why that person likes these material possessions in a more exaggerated way than other people do. We can't be condescending about this person, even if we'd rather like to be. What we can do is make sure they get their come-uppance. But, if you are cynical about your characters, that cynicism will infect everything you write. And whatever else you do, you mustn't despise them. If you want to despise anybody, there are plenty of people in the real world who are more worthy of your disapprobation.

Often, villains will be more than just the sum of their villainy. After all, Fagin may run a gang of child thieves and he may spend a great deal too much time thinking about all the rings, brooches, bracelets and watches that he's accumulating in his little box, but he has redeeming features too. He looks after his boys better than they're looked after in the workhouse — undoing the embroidered lettering on pocket handkerchiefs beats picking oakum. And, in his own roundabout way, Fagin teaches them a trade — pickpocketing.

If we think about the circumstances in which people live, what motivates them, why they act as they do, what is going through their minds, then we can create both monstrous villains as well as minor-key antagonists, designed to stand in the way of your protagonist as they strive towards their goal.

## Over to you

The seven deadly sins are:

- Envy
- Gluttony

- Greed
- Lust
- Pride
- Sloth
- Wrath

Write a scene in which a character displays one of these sins. Perhaps attempt the exercise twice. Once with an out-and-out villain. The second time with a character who is unlikeable, rather than entirely villainous.

# Postscript

Well, that's a dance through some of the aspects of character creation. Thank you for reading this far, or shame on you for skipping to the back pages.

Here's a good place to reiterate that there is no formula for character creation, nor is there one single method. There's also a certain falsehood in trying to set down on paper a process as elusive as this, where we're trying to recreate living human beings to inhabit your imaginary world. This is made even harder by the fact that no two writers I spoke to took the same approach. However, what they all did say was that character is vital. The writer's goal of creating vibrant, living beings is the same no matter what approach you take, it's just your means of getting there will be very different.

I hope what you've read here has been useful and enjoyable. I fully realise that not everything in these pages will have been relevant to you, but feel free to cherry-pick what you think might work for you.

I'll just leave you with this little thought as a kind of summary.

There are essentially 6 main ways in which the writer can convey character:

1. Physical description. What your character looks like, how they move, etc.
2. What you, as the author tell us about this character, usually filtered through a narrative voice.
3. What your characters does.
4. What your character thinks.
5. What your character says.
6. What other characters in the story say about them. And possibly what they think about them, if we are writing

something from several viewpoints.

To this, you might also add a possible seventh: that a character also comes alive indirectly, through other elements, such as setting or the very people with whom they mix.

Good luck with your writing.

# Bibliography

## Novels, Plays and Stories

Amis, Kingsley. *Lucky Jim*.

Amis, Martin. *Money*.

Austen, Jane. *Pride and Prejudice*.

Banks, Iain. *The Wasp Factory*.

Barnes, Julian. *Arthur and George*.

Boyne, John. *The Boy in the Striped Pyjamas*.

Brecht, Bertholt. *Life of Galileo, Mother Courage and Her Children*.

Brontë, Emily. *Wuthering Heights*.

Brown, Dan. *The Da Vinci Code*.

Bukowski, Charles. *Ham on Rye, Factotum, Women*.

Bunyan, John. *The Pilgrim's Progress*.

Camus, Albert. *The Outsider*.

Carey, Peter. *True History of the Kelly Gang*.

Céline. *Journey to the End of the Night*.

Chandler, Raymond. *The Big Sleep*.

Charters, Ann. *The Story and Its Writer — an Introduction to Short Fiction*.

Conan Doyle, Arthur. *The Sherlock Holmes stories*.

Cooper, Jilly. *The Rutshire Chronicles* series.

Cunningham, Michael. *The Hours*.

Defoe, Daniel. *Robinson Crusoe*.

Dexter, Colin. *The Inspector Morse* novels.

Dickens, Charles. *David Copperfield*.

Durrell, Lawrence. *The Alexandria Quartet*.

Eliot, George. *Middlemarch*.

Eugenides, Jeffrey. *The Virgin Suicides*.

Faulkner, William. *Absalom, Absalom!*

Fitzgerald, F. Scott. *The Great Gatsby*.

Flaubert, Gustave. *Madame Bovary*.

Fleming, Ian. *The James Bond* books.

Fuentes, Carlos. *Diana: the Goddess who Hunts Alone.*

Gary, Romain. *White Dog.*

Graves, Robert. *I, Claudius; They Hanged My Saintly Billy.*

Greene, Graham. *Brighton Rock.*

Grossmith, George & Weedon. *Diary of a Nobody.*

Haddon, Mark. *The Curious Incident of the Dog in the Night-time.*

Hardy, Thomas. *The Return of the Native, Tess of the D'Urbervilles.*

Harris, Thomas. *The Silence of the Lambs.*

Heller, Joseph. *Catch-22.*

Heller, Zoë. *Notes on a Scandal.*

Highsmith, Patricia. *The Talented Mr. Ripley* and sequels.

Huxley, Aldous. *Brave New World.*

Ishiguro, Kazuo. *The Remains of the Day.*

Jones, Lloyd. *The Book of Fame.*

Kerouac, Jack. *On the Road.*

Larsson, Stieg. *The Girl with the Dragon Tattoo.*

Lawrence, D. H. *Lady Chatterley's Lover.*

Lee, Harper. *To Kill a Mockingbird.*

Mamet, David. *Speed-the-Plow.*

Mantel, Hilary. *Wolf Hall.*

McCarthy, Cormac. *The Road.*

McEwan, Ian. *Enduring Love.*

Melville, Herman. *Moby Dick.*

Molière. *Le Malade Imaginaire.*

O'Brien, Tim. *The Things They Carried* (Short story in collection of same name).

Ondaatje, Michael. *The English Patient.*

Orwell, George. *1984, Animal Farm.*

Plath, Sylvia. *The Bell Jar.*

Pratchett, Terry. *The Discworld series.*

Rowling, J.K . *The Harry Potter series.*

Sachar, Louis. *Holes.*

Salinger, J. D. *The Catcher in the Rye.*

Shakespeare, William. *Macbeth, Romeo & Juliet, A Midsummer*

*Night's Dream, Othello, Hamlet, King Lear.*

Shields, Carol. *Larry's Party.*

Spiegelman, Art. *Maus.*

Thurber, James. *The Secret Life of Walter Mitty.*

Toole, John Kennedy. *A Confederacy of Dunces.*

Vonnegut, Kurt. *Galapagos.*

Waterhouse, Keith. *Billy Liar.*

Waugh, Evelyn. *Scoop.*

Welsh, Irvine. *Filth.*

Williford, Lex & Martone, Michael (eds). *The Scribner Anthology of Contemporary Short Fiction.*

## Films and TV Series

*Annie Hall,* feature film directed by Woody Allen.

*Bienvenue Chez les Ch'tis,* feature film directed by Dany Boon.

*Fawlty Towers,* BBC TV Series.

*Jaws,* feature film directed by Steven Spielberg.

*Lincoln,* feature film directed by Steven Spielberg.

*Little Britain,* BBC TV Series.

*My Left Foot,* feature film directed by Jim Sheridan.

*One Foot in the Grave,* BBC TV series.

*Only Fools and Horses,* BBC TV series.

*Psycho,* feature film directed by Alfred Hitchcock.

*Rear Window,* feature film directed by Alfred Hitchcock.

*Rififi,* feature film directed by Jules Dassin.

*Star Wars,* feature film directed by George Lucas

*The Beiderbecke Affair,* Yorkshire TV series (written by Alan Plater).

*The Carry On films,* series of feature films.

*The Fast Show,* BBC TV Series.

*The Italian Job,* feature film directed by Peter Collinson.

*The Omen,* feature film directed by Richard Donner.

*The Phil Silvers Show,* CBS TV series.

*The Simpsons,* Fox TV series.

*Top Cat*, Hanna-Barbera Productions.

## Music
Costello, Elvis. *Satellite* (from the album Spike).
Gilbert, W.S. and Sullivan, Arthur. *The Gondoliers.*

## Books on Writing and Literature and Other Relevant Matters

Ackerman, Angela & Puglisi, Becca. *The Emotion Thesaurus: A Writer's Guide to Character Expression.*
Aitken, Rosemary. *Writing a Novel — A Practical Guide.*
Allott, Miriam. *Novelists on the Novel.*
Anderson, Linda & Neale, Derek. *Creative Writing – A Workbook with Readings.*
Angwin, Roselle. *Creative Novel Writing.*
Aristotle. *Poetics.*
Atwood, Margaret. *Negotiating with the Dead — A Writer on Writing.*
Bell, Julia & Magrs, Paul. *The Creative Writing Coursebook.*
Boylan, Clare. *The Agony and the Ego — The Art and Strategy of Fiction Writing Explored.*
Braine, John. *How to Write a Novel.*
Brande, Dorothea. *Becoming a Writer.*
Burroway, Janet & Stuckey-French, Elizabeth. *Writing Fiction — A Guide to Narrative Craft.*
Cuddon, J. A. *The Penguin Dictionary of Literary Terms and Literary Theory.*
Edelstein, Linda N. *Writer's Guide to Character Traits.*
Egri, Lajos. *The Art of Dramatic Writing.*
Faulks, Sebastian. *Faulks on Fiction.*
Forster, E. M. *Aspects of the Novel.*
Frey, James N. *How to Write a Damn Good Novel.*
Gardner, John. *The Art of Fiction — Notes on Craft for Young Writers.*

George, Elizabeth. *Write Away.*

Graham, Robert; Newall, Helen; Leach, Heather & Singleton, John. *The Road to Somewhere.*

James, P. D. *Talking about Detective Fiction.*

King, Stephen. *On Writing — A Memoir.*

Kress, Nancy. *Characters, Emotion and Viewpoint; Dynamic Characters.*

Lamott, Anne. *Bird by Bird — Some Instructions on Writing and Life.*

Leder, Meg; Hefron, Jack & the editors of Writer's Digest. *The Complete Handbook of Novel Writing.*

Lodge, David. *The Art of Fiction.*

Maisel, Eric & Maisel, Ann. *What Would Your Character Do? Personality Quizzes for Analyzing Your Characters.*

McKee, Robert. *Story.*

Mullan, John. *How Novels Work.*

Newman, Jenny; Cusick, Edmond & La Tourette, Aileen. *The Writer's Workbook.*

Newman, Sandra & Mittelmark, Howard. *How Not to Write a Novel.*

Phillips, Larry. *Ernest Hemingway on Writing.*

Plimpton, George. *Writers at Work, The Paris Review Interviews.* There are several different series available.

Prose, Francine. *Reading Like a Writer.*

Randall, Rona. *Writing Popular Fiction.*

Roberts, James; Mitchell, Barry & Zubrinich, Roger (Eds). *Writers on Writing.*

Schmidt, Victoria Lynn. *45 Master Characters.*

Scofield, Sandra. *The Scene Book — A Primer for the Fiction Writer.*

Seger, Linda. *Creating Unforgettable Characters.*

Singleton, John. *The Creative Writing Workbook.*

Stanislavski, Konstantin. *An Actor Prepares; Building a Character.*

Swift, Graham. *Making an Elephant — Writing from Within.*

Theophrastus, transl. J.M. Edmonds. *The Characters of*

*Theophrastus*

Vogler, Christopher. *The Writer's Journey — Mythic Structure for Storytellers and Screenwriters.*

Wall, Geoffrey. *Flaubert: A Life.*

Wood, James. *How Fiction Works.*

## Other Resources

American Psychiatric Association. *Diagnostic and Statistical Manual of Mental Health Disorders.*

Cohen, Nick. *You Can't Read This Book — Censorship in an Age of Freedom.*

Fox, Kate. *Watching the English.*

Halliwell, Leslie. *Halliwell's Film Guide.*

Ronson, Jon. *The Psychopath Test.*

**COMPASS**
**BOOKS**

Compass Books focuses on practical and informative 'how-to' books for writers. Written by experienced authors who also have extensive experience of tutoring at the most popular creative writing workshops, the books offer an insight into the more specialised niches of the publishing game.